ADVANCE PRAISE

I have read most all Dr. Robert Newton's fiction books and I am fascinated by his shift to a non-fiction work that both enlightens and entertains with his integration of philosophy and history. *The Immortality Prophecy* investigates the possibility of living forever—and whether we should even aspire to such a goal. Newton makes a powerful argument for immorality yet caused me to ponder if our preoccupation with defying mortality is the very key that has driven civilization.

One could propose since the dawn of mankind the deepest quest in life has been to find immortality; throughout history wars have been waged as people chose what they believed the right path. Newton's books provide eye-opening possibilities, which may compel humans to keep moving forward in this lofty pursuit.

Newton's subtitle starts the journey: *Let the Reveal Begin!* He teases out myriad possibilities and engages readers in a number of mind-bending facets of securing immortality—and the implications thereof should we be able to acquire an impeccable, disease-free body. He challenges readers to look deeper, engage more fully, and continue to question how the journey plays into the direction and survival of civilization. Readers will find the book a deeply satisfying one... optimistic about the human condition and insightful about the turns the pursuit for immortality has made in history.

A. Stearns, BSBAM, MAOM
Life Coach 4-Dimensional Success

The Immortality Prophesy is a book that takes a complex subject, immortalizing the human body, and breaks it down into an understandable form; bringing me to believe it just might be possible to do what Dr. Newton suggests. As a nurse, I find his breathairian concept of nutrifying a body without food very foreign to what I have been taught, yet he scientifically supports just how this can be/is done. The concept that we can create energy to sustain ourselves is mind blowing, but I must say Dr. Newton fully substantiates his points. The book can be the grist upon which we may start looking at our human bodies in a vastly different light, and what type of lifespans we may attain.

Bertha Eloina Nash, LVN
Compassionate Care

Robert J. Newton writes on a wide range of philosophical, ethical and scientific subjects. In a long line of publications, his book, *The Immortality Prophecy* is a detailed gleaning of his fifty-plus years of engaging in education, experience and enlightenment on a sensitive topic.

Newton's newest release is a meticulously argued, and perceptively written book. His intent is to describe what he has discovered as methods prolonging physical life via medical and technological means. The author demonstrates in a clear, intelligent style how each concept he discusses impacts society and decisions made in a quest for immortality.

Newton, a philosopher, scientist and logician, uses scientific evidence to assess the chances of immortality being true—defying those who claim they are almost certainly false. He would contend our every-thought... every consciousness... life itself... is dependent on the body. Seeking to extend the conscious experiences we have as the totality of our lives, Newton reflects on death as a term defining the limits and boundaries on them. It quickly becomes evident Newton believes spiritual and philosophical leanings are sufficient as a defense against life's pain or potential ending.

It is also evident Newton cares deeply about his family, friends, neighbors, and about those who perish in wars, genocides, and natural disasters, and that at some level he finds the idea of a godless universe agonizing. Not knowing truly what comes after death, Newton's guess is as good as anyone's. A thoughtful and challenging author, however, his book will find its way to the hands of those who will agree fully with his every precept; while others may reject his work in anger and dismay or refuse to read it all together. There will also be a camp of readers willing to accept the evidence of science, yet others who, although accepting that evidence and believing the Universe is divinely created, will find much that will infuriate or frustrate. However, what Newton does is forces each to think about personal beliefs... both the "what" and the "why" of them—and that is never a bad thing.

T.R. Stearns, EdS
Retired Superintendent of Schools, Educator, Editor

———————◇◇◇◇———————

Let us rejoice for the vitality that comes from the secrets and controversial secret teachings being shared and taught by Dr. Robert Newton, especially in his book series.

The understanding and wisdom, which has been shared through Dr. Robert Newton's book, *The Immortality Prophecy*, is an intentional 'Stroke of Insight' in a good way.

Reverend David H. Roscher, CHt.
Empowerment & Holistic Health Coach
Http://About.me/dynamicDavid http://dynamicDavid.me

THE IMMORTALITY PROPHECY

LET THE REVEAL BEGIN!

THE IMMORTALITY PROPHECY

LET THE REVEAL BEGIN!

BY

Dr. Robert J. Newton, J.D., N.D.

Beyond the Bounds of Earth Publishing,

Entertainment and Education

Great Motivational Talks

The Immortality Prophecy

Title ID: 6133883

PRINT: ISBN-13: 978-0996137133

ISBN-10: 0996137130

DIGITAL: 978-0-9961371-6-4

Dr. Robert J. Newton
20253 Evening Breeze Dr.
Walnut, California 91789

http://www.drrobertnewton.com/

Ordering Information:
Quantity sales. Special discounts are available on quantity purchases by corporations, associations, and others. For details, contact the publisher at the address above.

Printed in the United States of America
First Edition

14 13 12 11 10 / 10 9 8 7 6 5 4 3 2 1

| Dedication

This book is dedicated to:

Every person who has realized, or will eventually conclude—there is much more to God, the planet Earth, and us... than has been reliably revealed to humankind.

Anyone who is eager to pierce a disturbing veil of ignorance and suppression of the true nature of life and immortality, which became the focus of my first book—*Pathways to God: Experiencing the Energies of the Living God in Our Everyday Life*—followed by a cutting edge treatise on natural healing: *A Map to Healing and Your Essential Divinity Through Theta Consciousness*.

Readers who are more inclined to engage in a controversial topic through a series of revealing fictional accounts as found in my subsequent publications:

> **The Hidden Codes of God**: *A Journey to the Unknown Secrets and Dimensions of the Divine and the Energy of Love*
>
> **Beyond the Mists of Time**: *When Trees Ruled the Earth*
>
> *In Search of the Body Immortal: Let the Journey Begin*
>
> **Planet of the Stupids**: *Bringing Back the Light of God to Planet Earth and Creating a Paradise Found.*

Persons seeing a deeper level of consciousness, and interested the most cutting edge information on health, life extension and the immortality of the human body; readers who want to increase their awareness through scientific findings and age-old esoteric information.

Writing this book was a great learning experience for me; a joyous endeavor. I hope it is the same for readers and reviewers of this book!

Namaste,
Shalom,

Dr. Robert J. Newton, 4-2-16

Chet Resh Hey

הֵרֶח

If you were to destroy the belief in immortality in mankind, not only love but every living force on which the continuation of all life in the world depended, would dry up at once.

~ Fyodor Dostoevsky (1821–1881)
Russian Novelist

| TABLE OF CONTENTS

Getting Things Done To a More Radiant Us with a Pathway to Such.

Going a lot deeper with more to chew. What happens on the atomic level of creation and how do we reprogram our minds into a state of improved health and immortality?

Let me ask ye, do you want to be free and live like a tree? Then mantras might be for thee!

Dare we ask for more? Ask and ye shall receive, and in numbers shall we find colour!

Angel jive and new Angels arrive, so in angels our bodies may abide.

If we stop eating food, will we really be putting out body in a "fix" so we need to keep our chop sticks?

Are you ready for heaven, or in need of more leaven? Quartz crystals, Pyramids and leyline vortexes might just provide such!

Hallucinogenic, psychedelic, psychotropic substances, ormus and finding the body great–meaning–preparing the brain/mind to make the climb to bodily immortality.

Negative ions can make us feel fine, even when we are in a bind!

Hydrogen and oxygen—do these relate to prana again and breathairian protocols?

Getting off the wheel of karma and near death experiences. How long does it take before we go to heaven?

Into a summary we shall delve.

Now, are we ready to be weaned from a human body and assume our divine genes? Remember the foundation of all creation, the atom, is 99.5% massless.

LIST OF FIGURES—

| ACKNOWLEDGEMENTS—

The Immortality Prophesy follows my recently published, *In Search of the Body Immortal: Let the Journey Begin.* The latter book, a novel, was filled with many factual things which showed how the character therein, James, followed many clues to immortalize his human body. Upon the urging of my brilliant editor, Anna Weber of **Voices in Print Publishing**, to write a non-fiction book on immortality, it seemed a logical progression to me. Little did I know, just how much new, breakthrough information I would be receiving for this new book. So... first and foremost, I need to thank Anna for positing the idea for this book, as well as her extreme competence in bringing all my books together into published form.

I also am still deeply indebted to my deceased wife, **Charlette Newton Smith**, for being my best friend, lover and teacher, extraordinaire. The major thing that really animates my research and my writing is my highly developed intuition, which I use in a number of ways—including remote viewing into the past and future, and my ability to access information stored in the atomic field of the Universe, known in *The Vedas* as The Akashic Records (knowledge from the skies) and in Patanjali's, *The Yoga Sutras* as "Celestial Hearing." These abilities became more finely honed after I learned the three legs of Kriya Kundalini Yoga, especially Kriya

Kundalini Pranayam(a). The ironic thing about this is that I almost did not learn the Kriya Kundalini Yoga protocols and only did after great insistence by Charlette. Although she left Earth almost three years ago, I regularly communicate with her from the higher dimensions of Heaven. So I am fortunate to continue with her counsel.

Additionally, I am greatly aided by my fiancé, **Bertha Eloina Nash**, who keeps our household running smoothly and who also is an extremely loving presence. I might have discovered that Love is fundamentally light yet she just loves unconditionally, which may reveal functional knowledge is more useful than knowledge of the academic type. I freely admit Eloina gets ignored quite a bit since when I am on the scent of a new concept or immersed in writing about that concept. I am oblivious to everything except my immediate task at hand. I have a caveat for people considering get involved with a prolific writer: *You might want to avoid such a relationship, as it can be frustrating for the non-writing partner!*

The greatest blessing in my life, other than the reunion with my deceased soulmate, Charlette Newton Smith, is being initiated into the science of Kriya Kundalini Yoga as dispensed by Kriya Yoga Satguru (guru of gurus), **Babaji Nagaraj**. I am sure I practiced Kriya Kundalini Pranayam(a) in other lifetimes but to have the inner guidance of an avatar is a blessing of blessings. Babaji dictated his book to V.T. Neelakantan and Yogi S.A.A. Ramaiah, *The Death of Death*. We could be going beyond this in this text.

Yogi Marshall **Govindan Satchidananda**, who is found at www.babajiskriyayoga.net/, initiated me into the highest levels of Kriya Kundalini Yoga and I am grateful for this needed initiation, even though without knowing it, I was actually doing Kriya Kundalini Pranayam, ten years before I was initiated into such. Yogi Satchidananda has devoted almost fifty years of his life to disseminating Kriya Kundalini Yoga to the world under the original auspices of Yogi, S.S.A. Ramaiah and his guru, the venerated Babaji Nagaraj, the acknowledged head of Kriya Kundalini Yoga. I also teach the Kriya Kundalini Yoga protocols you can find on my website: www.drrobertnewton.com

I have also been blessed to have the counsel of Kriya Kundalini Satguru/Avatar, **Patanjali**, through his book, *The Yoga Sutras*. This is a concise exposition and explanation of Kriya Kundalini Yoga.

An invaluable source for me has been ***The Bhagavad Gita***, which is one of the chapters of *The Mahabarata*. There is much source material that relates to creating an immortal body—more than you would find anywhere else.

I also need to thank **Mary Baker Eddy**, who wrote the definitive book on Christian healing and immortality, *Science and Health with Key to the Scriptures*. As a result of reading this book, since 1961 I have fervently believed our bodies do not need to die and that a state of Heaven can exist on Earth. Only recently, have I accumulated the scientific knowledge, which shows these ideas are not the lunatic rantings of a deluded and diminished mind.

I would also like to thank **Dr. J. J. Hurtak** and his break through book, *The Keys of Enoch*. He discussed many concepts in this book before anyone else was talking about them, including us creating an immortalized body of light... a Merkaba(h), the importance of ATP (Adeno triphosphate) in creating fuel for an immortalized body and the idea of a Cosmic Computer in the center of the Universe where the knowledge of everything that has ever happened in the Universe is stored and accessible.

Further, I am indebted to the insights in the research of **Dr. Gerald Pollack** and his research into the importance of Hydrogen in creating, EZ-water, H_3O_2 and ATP (a biochemical way to store and use energy). What Pollack did was reveal a non-caloric, non-glucose and non- glycolysis way to make the ATP that fuels our bodies through oxidative phosphorylation. This also explains how people can live a vibrant life without eating food, known as Breathairianism.

Peter Arthur Straubinger produced the documentary, *In the Beginning There was Light* and has been a guest on my radio show, *The Dr. Robert J. Newton Show* on the Artist First Radio Network. It was leads he gave me, which ultimately led me to scientific proof of how the breathairian protocol is, in fact, achievable.

I would also like to thank **T. R. Stearns** for his cogent and insightful reviews of my past books. The astute former educator actually sees things in my books I do not and so he teaches me in the process of his reviews. Thank you, so much!

Thanks to the *American Journal of Clinical Nutrition* for publishing **Dr. Paul Webb 's** research findings that 23% of the energy in our bodies comes from a source beyond the body itself. Thanks also to Dr. Webb for his diligence and belief in completing his research.

Also, a deep gratitude goes to **J. V. G. A. Durnin**, the Scottish nutritionist, well-noted for his research in the field of human nutrition and energetics of human metabolism—for his research on calories—and **William Riggins** for the same, which he shares in his book, *The Myth of the Calorie*.

Albert Szent-Györgyi I thank for completing research that indicates the more Hydrogen present in our bodies… the more energy we have.

This also dovetails with the research of Australian Decathlon champion, **John O'Neill**, who has discovered he can increase the length of his workout without the adverse effects of lactic acid build up by increasing the amount of Hydrogen present in his body.

I acknowledge the many discoveries of French radiesthesist, **André Bovis**, who conducted research into the effects and benefits of pyramid energies. Dr. Bovis also created *The Bovis Scale*, which measures the energy in food, and the pyramid form, which directs us toward those foods that optimally nutrify us, and reflect where the most powerful points are located inside and outside of a pyramid.

Other pyramid researchers I want to acknowledge include: Dr. Fred Bell, author of *The of Ignorance*; Bill

Kerell; J. Davidovits; Doug Benjamin; Christopher Dunn, who wrote *Giza Pyramid Plant, Dr*. Patrick Flanagan, author of *Pyramid Power;* Dr. Sulejman Redzic; Janez Pelko; and Dr. Carl Benedicks. Their research and collective wisdom was most invaluable in the writing of this book.

My gratitude also goes out to my friend, **Dr. Juan Acosta**, neurological researcher, who shared his experiences of subject's brainwaves in mind altering drugs like Ayahuasca, Psilocybin etc. and brainwave tomography reflecting changes experienced during sexual orgasm.

I also express my appreciation to **Dr. Jeremy Narby**, anthropologist and author of *The Cosmic Serpent: DNA and the Origins of Knowledge*. I count this as one of the best books on the subject of altered states of consciousness experienced under the influence of Ayahuasca. It also reveals how the DNA sequence was discovered by what are considered primitive Indians—200 years before our contemporary scientists.

Much thanks, likewise, to **Barry Carter**, who has twice been on my radio show, *The Dr. Robert J. Newton Show: Real Conspiracies with Scientific and Spiritual Solutions*, on the Artist First Radio Network, to share his keen knowledge of Monatomic Gold (Ormus White Gold), and how it can extend our lives and put us into altered brainwaves of Alpha and Theta.

I am indebted, as well, to the ancient Arabic Alchemists, as well as European Alchemists... especially Roger Bacon, Sir Francis Bacon and Sir Isaac Newton, among others. Their knowledge of Alchemy, along with that of Dr. Paul Foster Case and his group, The Builders of the Adytum, have the knowledge necessary to add indispensible pieces to the immortality puzzle.

Thanks to **Drs. Krueger and Sulman** for extensive research into negative ions and their health benefits and commensurate consciousness expanding abilities.

Thanks to the **myriad researchers** who revealed how the telomere in our chromosomes function… and how telomerase enzyme is like a "fountain of youth" that keep these telomere from wearing out, which ultimately leads to our bodies being able to access an immortalized status.

My deep gratitude goes to Soviet-born American author, **Zechariah Sitchin**, who decoded the Anunaki Sumerian language and revealed much to us about the extended life spans of which we are capable of living. His books include, among others, *When Time Began* and *The 12th Planet*.

I acknowledge of the work of **Annie Paden** and **David Judd** that revealed how light photons stimulate the Pineal gland and the human body.

A long time ago I procured a copy of **Stephen Chiang's** book, *The Tao of Sexuality: The Book of Infinite Wisdom* and **Mantak Chia's** book, *The Taoist Secrets of Love: Cultivating Male Sexual Energy*. What is invaluable for me about these books is how they illuminate a path to immortality through a Taoist sexual energy approach.

I am privileged to have found another amazing book, which was translated by **Jane Huang** that opened my mind to the use of breathing canons or various breathing meditations: *Primordial Breath: An Ancient Chinese Way of Prolonging Life Through Breath Control.*

The study by **Nithyananda Sangha**, *Scientific Study of Kundalini Activation and its Benefits*, helped me to understand how Kundalini Yoga energizes the human body as revealed by MTT Cell Analysis.

| INTRODUCTION

Attention, readers… you owe it to yourself to read the Introduction thoroughly, since it sets the stage for the premise and information presented throughout the book.

In *The New Testament* of *The Bible,* Jesus (Yeshua), prophesized, "Greater works than these shall ye do also." Other than Christian Scientists, who have often been exposed to this in *Science and Health with Key to the Scriptures,* by Mary Baker Eddy, nary a Christian I have met understands what this means. In fact, I would say it has been deliberately ignored so as to perpetuate the idea that mankind is inherently flawed; inherent sinners can only find redemption for this by confessing their sins and accepting Jesus Christ as their savior and Lord and Master. In contravention to this, when you consult the Gnostic Christian Texts, from *The Nag Hamadhi Documents,* detailed in William Henry's, *The Secrets of Sion,* you do not find the sinner scenario at all. This is the large "pink Elephant" in the room perceived only by a very few souls, yet nevertheless a large presence rather hard to ignore.

Irrespective of this, what Jesus was telling us in *The New Testament* was we could exceed his works, and since Jesus in fact transcended death and took this body into an immortalized state of light, he was prophesying we would do this and even more! Why we have not been taught that will be explained shortly, herein. It is evident the church who proclaims to be the keeper of Jesus' words, The Roman Catholic Church, seems to have gone out its way to do otherwise and to distort and/or cover up our Divine heritage from our Creator (please refer to *Catholicism AKA The Holy Roman Catholic Church*). This is proclaimed neither with anger nor malice, but it is difficult to come to another conclusion, considering the information conveyed by Jesus in *The Nag Hamadhi Documents,* also known as *The Gnostic Texts.* The Protestant churches have been complicit in this by not questioning things that could be dubious and thus also leading us off the cliff of death, as it were, and the puny life spans that have resulted from the ignorance of our true nature.

In *The Corpus Hermetica/Hermeticum,* Thoth/ Hermes/Enoch tells us, "Focus your mind—I will teach you. You must understand that which is within you, which sees and hears, is divine awareness itself and that the highest consciousness inside you is nothing other than Supreme Reality. There is no difference between your innermost being and God. Experience the light of your consciousness and realize what it really is. Those who remember their real nature attain the greatest good. Knowing they come from a world of light, they return to that immortal light. But those who prefer the life of the body become lost and confused and subject to death. Why have you surrendered to death, you men and women who are capable of immortality? Wake up! Stop your ignorant behavior, step out of the shadows and claim your birthright—everlasting divine awareness ".

Most amazing is all of this… because the information is related by an ancient figure, regarded with great reverence in ancient Sumer/Sumeria as Thoth, Atlantis as Tehuti, Egypt as Thoth, Greece as Hermes, Palestine as Enoch, Central America as Quetzalcoatl, and Merlin in England. It has been related in the Jewish tradition that Enoch was so favored by God that he was asked to join God in the Heavens on *The Tree of Life,* next to the Arch Angel Michael/Mickel and he actually ascended into the heavens in a column of light. So this exalted soul has basically revealed our true nature as light, and this light is the key to immortalizing our bodies on Planet Earth; we do not have to cast off our body of Earth to become immortalized beings. This is as profound as what Jesus shared with us, albeit much more verbose, yet such verboseness is very specific of our true nature, which sadly has been obscured from our view and quite deliberately, to wit.

In John 12:36 Jesus said, "Believe in the Light while you have the light so you can become children of the light." In John 8:12, it is revealed… and Jesus spoke to them, saying "I am the light of the world; he who follows me will not walk in darkness, but have the Light of life."

In this book, you will learn the prime importance of Light, and notice how it is capitalized here and in the Biblical scripture, because a capital "Light" would signify the Creator itself or some force of an incredible magnitude, possibly much beyond our limited human perspective of this. This Light is also a part of the Kabala in the Merkaba/Merkabah, which describes an immortalized body of light. In Hebrew, "mer" means a connecting thread of light, "ka" means spirit and "ba" means body/a chariot of God. Hence, we have a light, spirit body, which goes back thousands of years in the Hebrew traditions.

Also, the idea of humans being inherent sinners and not worthy of an immortalized body on Earth has at least two major flaws. First, the genesis of the word "sin" means "to miss" and "forgetfulness" and I would add, an "ignorance" of our divine origins. Secondly, what kind of God would condemn us to be sinners because of the acts of our ancestors, notably, Adam and Eve? That would be one angry God, most likely whom we could never satisfy except upon our death! Where does the "loving God" fit into this? A retributive God could not be a loving God! This something I realized when I was just five years old, in 1951, as Pastor Robert Roland, was yelling at me in his sermon… that I was going to hell if I did not repent and accept Jesus Christ as my Lord and Master. I did not have a problem with the Lord and Master part, just that I could be sent to hell for not repenting when I was being taught in Sunday School in 1 John 4:16 *"God is Love and those who abide in Love, abide in God and God abides in Them"*.

In light of this, as it were, living life on Earth in these circumstances would be an exercise in futility. In Chapter Eight of *In Search of the Body Immortal: Let the Journey Begin,* the author reveals the real meaning of the word Love, which equates to light, in a numeral evaluation/computation, and which is also referred to as Gematria, a system of code and numerology adopted into Jewish culture, which assigns numerical values to words or phrases. Gematria is also intertwined into the Hermetic traditions, as well

In a direct manner, this circles us back to *The Corpus Hermeticum* and Jesus' thoughts and the factors of light and immortality referred to, therein. Continually, throughout this treatise, you will be given the opportunity to see just how things fit together in regard to the immortalizing of our human bodies! There is a Divine Plan to all of this and it is polytheistic and poly-scientific and poly-esoteric, which means there is not one religion, branch of science or branch of esoteric knowledge that completely explains the immortality puzzle other than Taoism and Kriya Kundalini Yoga, and even these traditions receive more illumination from science and other esoteric traditions.

People really need to re-consider the whole idea of sin and sinners. A sinner is simply someone who has forgotten their divine origins. In *The 72 Names of God: Technology for the Soul*, Rabbi Yehuda Berg explains when we descended to Earth from Heaven, we were already living in a state of perfection and light and yet we agreed to play a game on Earth, whereby the knowledge of our perfection would be hidden from us and the goal of the game is to search out and find that perfection, here on Earth. This is another way of saying we are not these inherently flawed and evil beings. Why should our ignorance of this be punishable at law or by our Creator/God? Would most parents punish their children for being forgetful... for being ignorant? That would be ludicrous, would it not? So this is like a watershed moment; either we can continue being slaves to religions and governments, who proclaim they are here to help us or we can *... break on through to the other side,* as Jim Morrison of The Doors sang about decades ago, in "Break on Through (To the Other Side)."

The seventh name of God, from "The 72 Names of God" from "Exodus" 14, vs. 19-21, of *The Torah,* is *Aleph Kaf Aleph,* which means restoring things to their perfect state. The 59th Name of God is *Hey Resh Chet,* meaning connected to the light. These two names, individually and collectively, mean you have been created perfectly and from light, not from the dust of the Earth or from a rib of a man, and that you are a perfect creation, formulated from photons that manifest the phenomena of light from the electromagnetic radiation emanating from atoms. These "72 Names of God" most likely predate *The Torah,* itself, by more than 400,000 years, originating from the Anunaki/Sumerians in Sumer and believed by some to be formulated by Enki and/or Thoth. Light is designated as Agna in *The Bhagavad Gita,* on page 369 of the Paramahansa Yogananda translation from Sanskrit to English. More scientific evidence and proof of these things will be provided in the text of this book, in Chapter One and elsewhere. There are number/numeral dynamics (Gematria) related to all of this that will be discussed in Chapter Four.

Isn't it interesting how the factor of light has appeared thrice now, including Jesus' statements, *The 72 Names of God,* and in Hermes' declaration in *The Corpus Hermeticum*? All of these allusions to light have been staring us in the face for millennia yet neither our ancestors nor we have noticed, other than a few Yogis, Taoists or Alchemists The beginning of the Indian civilization can be ascertained by back counting the Indian cycles of time, known as Yugs or Yugas, as was done by Swami Saraswati in *The True History and Religion of India*. In so doing, he calculated the genesis of India at 1.9 billon years (please refer to *Beyond the Mists of Time: When Trees Ruled the Earth* for further substantiation on this point).

Therefore, from such an ancient civilization, we might expect to find many things not known elsewhere in the Earth history, regarding ancient, forgotten, ignored and deliberately suppressed knowledge, which has happened over a period of time. For sure, at its essence, Kriya Kundalini Yoga, dating back thousands and millions and billions of years ago, is devoted to bringing more light into the human body so as to unveil the true immortal potential of a body.

Referencing the light created by the sounds of *Aum/Om:* this light has electromagnetic properties with plus and minus charges, creating an alternating current, known in Yoga and Hinduism as **Prana** and in Taoism as **Chi** and these are literally the same energy that run/power electrical appliances. The source of *Prana* and *Chi,* is atoms, which just happen to be comprised of plus (protons) electrical charges and minus (electrons) electrical charges, previously mentioned. These two charges create the magic of electromagnetism or electricity. Additionally, these atoms never wear out; their form can be changed but never destroyed. This is inherent in Albert Einstein's "First Law of Thermodynamics," where distilled translates to: *Energy can neither be created nor destroyed*. Really this statement would be more properly stated as, $E=mc2$ and Leibnitz's $E=mv2$ and Dr. Newton's,

E=pa2 (Energy = prana x aum squared), which are more clearly defined in *A Map to Healing and Your Essential Divinity Through Theta Consciousness*. Also refer to Dr. Francoise Tibika; in her book, *Molecular Consciousness,* as to the non-destructible aspects of the atom(s) and the light attached thereto.

The reason for eliminating matter from the formula of life and creation is quite simple: **there is no matter! There exists only energy and spirit** and never has matter of any sort ever been detected in the most powerful atomic collider (CERN), in Hadron, Switzerland, which leads one to believe it will never be isolated as such! As bombastic as this statement might sound, consider all of this in the light, as it were, of this factual knowledge: *The particle of all creation, the atom, is 99.9% without mass. Yet an atom manifests light and energy, which can be detected and quantified.* Sir Isaac Newton described light as a stream of particles and today we know these same particles as photons, which has been documented as the result of electromagnetic radiation emitted by atoms.

If our atoms are basically mass less, it begs the question, **"How can they be comprised of matter?"** Thus it would naturally follow, neither can human bodies—including the cells therein nor any forms of creation—be designated as matter, but rather the indestructible light and energy of the substance less or material less atom that likewise emits a lot of light and energy. Another question, as well, that must be inevitably raised: **"Why is this not apparent since people die and things deteriorate?"** Who has not seen or yet experienced this reality? Even the author has watched many friends die, including his own beloved wife... wrapped lovingly in his arms! The answer to this will surprise many people yet, as succinctly explained, it will become clearer.

Realize this, however—in *Science and Health with Key to the Scriptures*, by Mary Baker Eddy, the author bluntly states the imperfect creation is an illusion, that everything is perfect, including our bodies. Comparable in Hinduism, we are taught the concept of "Maya" wherein we learn to recognize the illusions that keep us from seeing the perfect creation. From the *Upanishads,* in ancient India, we have Sat Atma, which is the non-material substance underlying our every changing Universe. Plato, the great Greek philosopher, wrote of the perfect forms behind all creation. If this is true, it naturally follows we are perfect and part of that perfection lies within a perfect, immortalized body! These things highly suggest we are not comprised of deteriorating matter, something we have never been told!

According to Quantum Mechanics, **we create the things we experience... everything that occurs and is manifested in our lives.** This is unquestionably, true despite the fact humans are quite adept at shifting blame—to God, the Devil, their parents, spouses, siblings, associates, and any number of antagonists or villains—for the things that happen in their lives. The subconscious, mortal mind goes out of its way to deflect responsibility for the unpleasant things that happen in our lives. Quite honestly, I spent the largest portion of my life doing just such, however, I later learned I was the creator of my life. So the bad news is: **we create the bad things**, such as accidents that happen, and even the sickness and disease that manifest in our lives. The better news: **we have control over what happens in our lives**, including our health, our success, and ultimately even our prosperity!

Welcome to the realm of Quantum Mechanics and the obscured reality on planet Earth!

To fully understand how good and bad things occur in our lives, we must first understand just how the subconscious or unconscious, mortal mind, or even brain-computer stores information. If you find it surprising the subconscious/brain is referred to as a computer, consider the following: it has been determined our brains are a computer, more complex and sophisticated than the best super computer ever created.

Our brain-computer is capable of accessing and storing more than 7 million pieces of separate information per second, 24 hours a day, 7 days a week, 365 days a year... ad infinitum.

It takes a super computer 40 hours to compute what the human brain can do in one minute. What we need to consider is that we are not even remotely living up to our mental potential and we acquire and store information even as we sleep. What this means then, is our thoughts and emotions are being filed in our brain-computer, continuously, and without fail. The same thing applies to the words and even emotions of other people, aside from our own.

To go even further, our brain-computers take the information—that has been programmed therein—and with great precision, over time manifests the things that occur in our lives. Add to this the programming from the DNA you inherit from your parents, relatives and ancestors and you should begin to see what you face in your daily life. Unfortunately, you live with myriad fields of information from governments, schools, religions and media. Even more unfortunate—each constantly feeds scientifically incorrect information into your brain-computers and commensurately causes you to create lives that do not fulfill your Divine potential. One of those Divine potentials is immortality... in the here and now on the Earthly plane.

Undoubtedly, there are people, religions, pharmaceutical companies, governments, corporations and the allopathic medical establishment—each who benefits to some degree when we are confused, sick and deteriorating—even if such deterioration is over a long period of time. In fact, when our deterioration or aging occurs over a long duration of time, these entities and organizations profit even more from our eventual demise! **Do things really have to end in our so called "demise?"** I would say no, in light, as it were, of the following from Teilhard de Chardin, the French idealist philosopher and Jesuit priest: *We are not human beings having a spiritual experience. We are spiritual beings having a human experience.* **Our real essence then is spirit, energy, light and vibration!** How the hell can that deteriorate and be extinguished, when the atoms that comprise these very things are indestructible, to wit?

In regard to religious deception—or maybe it is just confusion—the Roman Catholic Church liberally edited the Bible at both the First and Second Council(s) of Nicaea, with all overt references to reincarnation removed in *The New Testament* and in *The Old Testament (The Torah),* references to reincarnation have been largely ignored. The ramifications of these actions result in the reality that both Christians and Jews are completely ignorant to a stream of recurring lives from the same Soul/Monad. Mohammed discussed discarding an old body and taking on a new one in *The Koran/Quran.* Yet nary a Muslim seems to know this! Why? Most likely because it is easier to control Christians, Jews, and Mozlems when someone believes there is only one lifetime in which to live on Earth. Couple this with the money that is extorted from parishioners via church authorities who promise dispensation and a place in heaven for them, directly tied to the suggestion they contribute money to the various church organizations. Does all this lead us to consider the reasons, as were mentioned earlier, we have not been told we have the capacity and capability to exceed the works of Jesus?

It is essential to also address Hindus and Buddhists, where there is the acceptance of reincarnation, except the Buddhists belief comes with a little twist... you come back to Earth in a different body. Either way, you still have church authorities or priests, who still exercise their privilege to extort money from their parishioners, promising a better life in the here and now—and when a person returns to Earth. I would contend there is a trap set up in this reincarnation scheme. You may have heard the reference to "The Wheel of Karma," which promotes you have to live many lives, maybe two thousand or more, before you can get off "The Wheel of Karma" and attain enlightenment.

Why the Wheel of Karma concept is not true is covered in *In Search of the Body Immortal: Let the Search Begin.* In these pages, I am vulnerable and honestly admit: I was caught up in this "Wheel of Karma" concept, myself! Fortunately, I experienced an epiphany, and realized how we are truly trapped by this belief, in deep contravention to the seventh *Name of God, Aleph Kaf Aleph,* which, in Hebrew, means restoring things to their perfect state. A closer study would imply we are already perfect and in the light of same… make the idea of 2000 successive life times being necessary to purify ourselves to be worthy of enlightenment a rather suspect belief, and maybe even to a certain extent, quite unnecessary, except to control and scare people into buying dispensation or favor with God via church authorities or organizations. Stay with me, and we will delve more deeply into this in Chapter Eleven.

Even worse than the diametric opposites set up by religious authorities and organizations, nothing in the history of the Earth has been set up better to extort money from us than the allopathic medical system. This system, while outstanding for treating traumatic injuries, albeit extremely expensive in doing such, is an absolute failure at treating sickness and disease and the price you will pay for such treatment is not even remotely in relation to the benefits provided. Such benefits are only temporary because the medicines and the **treatments used only treat symptoms and not the causative factors.** Herbal, homeopathic, chiropractic and energy healing, on the other hand, do tend to target the causative factors of sickness and disease and are provided at a vastly cheaper price and usually in a more efficient and effective manner!

In general, the allopathic medical system uses medicines where the **active ingredient of a plant has been synthesized there from**; the process leaves the inherent buffering compounds of the plant discarded, and lead to a consistent result of iatrogenesis, or side effects that do not ultimately meet the medical goals of the patient. If you doubt such, just procure a *Physicians Desk Reference,* which lists all of today's allopathic medicines and research this yourself. What you will uncover is quite disconcerting, to most people, at least.

Additionally, there are other allopathic medicines like Viagra and Cialis, which are little more than the result of chemical manipulation, and have no relationship to any plant naturally occurring. It is bad enough said medicines have strayed from the fundamentals of Western Medicine set forth by two Greek personages: Asclepius (god of medicine in ancient Greek religion and mythology) and Hippocrates (long accepted as the founder of medicine as a rational science); worse still are the prices charged for such medicines.

This brings us to the Allopathic idiocy of Oncology, which uses the toxic metal cocktail of Chemotherapy to attempt to kill cancer cells, when it is known that at best, **said cocktail can only make cancer cells go into hiding but never kill them. Radiation treatment**, likewise, will definitely cause burns and damage to a body but again, said treatment **can only make cancer cells go into hiding but never kill them!** This brings us to the surgery of Oncology, where the removing of tumors, removes a body process of using tumors to collect the cancer cells. In many cases, **once the tumor is removed, the cancer proceeds to systemically spread throughout the human body**! Does this not make you wonder, "Why not detoxify the body to remove the metabolic toxins that are causing the cancer cells, in the first place?" For me, this kind of information inspires a real, duh moment!

Need we also inquire whether there are viable options to the three major oncology protocols? Indeed there are, including treatment with:

Ozone, Hydrogen Peroxide, H_3O_2 (EZ Water), ESIAC, cayenne and habanero peppers;

Gerson® Therapy, which is a natural treatment to activate the body's ability to heal itself through an organic, plant-based diet, raw juices, and natural supplements and coffee enemas;

Burzynskik Protocols, led by Polish-born Dr. Burzynskik whose use of antineoplastons has been especially beneficial for brain cancers of children;

Chelation, Aloe Vera, and the Grape Diet Protocols;

Richway Bio-mat protocols, which have been used in Japan, to use thermography (heating the body) to kill cancer cells,

Alkalizing the human body to a 7.1-7.3 Ph with foods and supplements;

Dr. Joanna Budwig protocols, where we see the use of low fat cottage cheese and raw, unrefined Flaxseed oil/Linseed oil;

not to mention Laetrile, Sound Signature Healing, Dinsbaugh Light Therapy and Photo Luminescence blood treatment, just to name a few.

Note: *Although there are no other validated references to Dinsbaugh other than my own... he never claimed to cure cancer, yet my deceased wife completed research to support that his belief in violet light therapy, has done so in many cases.*

These more wholistic treatments only cost a few hundred or thousands of dollars or less versus oncological approaches, many of which can cost tens of thousands of dollars to hundreds of thousand of dollars or more! These alternative treatments are also vastly more effective in ridding the body of the mutated cancer cells.

It is evident what we experience in the oncological approach is little more than a way to take huge sums of your money, impoverish you immensely and not deliver the promised results of a permanent cure.

The same can be said for patented medicines provided by pharmaceutical companies, which are obscenely expensive and never remove the causation of a sickness or disease; just suppress symptoms. So again... we pay a lot and get a little——actually very little, if anything—other than fleeting relief.

Let me be blunt. The allopathic medical system and its accompanying pharmaceutical/medicinal options are designed to generate obscene amounts of money and prey on the ignorance of the people on Earth. I fervently know we are bamboozled into believing we will be healed when healing in this manner rarely occurs. The industry as a whole wants us to be sick—and never really cured, because of the lucrative nature of illness. In the process, as a society we become enslaved, harnessed, and beholden—to a system synchronized with impoverishment. This reality may be a revelation for many people and most likely what has been shared will be unpalatable, but in most cases, and especially this one, ignorance is not bliss!

As has already been alluded, pharmaceutical medicines are extremely expensive and never remove the cause of any malady. So why would the Patient Protection and Affordable Care Act (PPACA), which was forced upon us as the Affordable Care Act (ACA) or, less affectionately known as *Obamacare*, by way of the United States federal statute signed into law by President Barack Obama on March 23, 2010, be considered a reliable model? Unfortunately, if one looks deeply, the evidence exists such laws are predicated by money the pharmaceutical companies contribute to re-election campaigns, PACS, and thus makes legislators and presidents beholden to "the hand that feeds them!" Additionally, the undeniable reality that many allopathic medicines are approved which have many deleterious side effects, indicate they are suspect at best and an outright fraud at worst.

Governments are another "can of worms." Although they proclaim they are here to serve us, actual experience would indicate governments by their very nature are here to control us, as I have explored more in depth in the manuscript, *Planet of the Stupids*. Government, dissected in Greek, is govern (to control) and ment (minds) or to control minds. In fact, you can decipher from the laws that in fact each tends to impose decrees and penalties and take our God given rights and constitutional liberties away, as well. It is more than interesting to note the world's governments have decreed—through legislation—the allopathic medical model as the one we are required to use. The model has been forced upon us... including vaccines that have toxins, tracking devices and nano-bot cells that cannibalize our bodies. The intent is obvious—as governments go out of their way to make herbal medicines harder to procure and prosecute parents in courts of law for using said herbal and alternative protocols—when the children become sick or die! The results would beg the question, "Why are doctors, hospitals and pharmaceutical companies not prosecuted in courts of law when their procedures and medicines lead to more sickness and/or death?"

Stunning is the irony of this dichotomy!

The answer to this, again: said companies contribute obscene amounts of money to candidates, through their PACS —medical imaging technology, which provides economical storage and convenient access to images from multiple modalities—and as such, are protected by being lucrative funding sources for political candidates! Politicians will not "bite the hand" that feeds them and will actually go out of their way to protect their benefactors through personal and legislative intervention with the Federal Drug Administration (FDA). In the United States of America exists a government controlled by corporations through the obscene amounts of money bestowed upon legislators to their PACs.

Now, let us look at the world's corporations, which history would support have three primary objectives:

1. The first objective is to hoard or monopolize resources and markets, as a precursor to then push up the price of everything we consume. Many times, through these monopolies, prices are increased… even though the cost of the resources or products has not escalated or even actually decreased.

2. This leads us to the second goal, which is to charge as much for something as is possible, which ultimately is made possible through the first objective

3. Third: Most corporations are not interested in—or concerned about—their products being safe for use or consumption. Having no conscience or remorse, there is no protection against the harm or illness that actually stems from certain products or protocols!

Bluntly put, our governments benefit when we are sick and debilitated, and the medical corporations make a lot more money when we more easily controlled.
The proof is there for the viewing

Thus far, I have encouraged you to consider how and why various institutions benefit by our being sick and slowly—or not so slowly—dying. There is a strong belief held by certain elitist people, our governments, and the rich businessmen, wielding a great deal of political influence, who control our governments. In certain settings, you may hear these people referred to as The Cabal or Illuminati, but regardless the label, you can be assured they want to "thin the herd" and eliminate many billions of people living on planet Earth. You owe it to yourself to become aware of two little known features: The Georgia Guidestones and Agenda 21.

Georgia Guidestones

The first is known as the Georgia Guidestones, which is a huge granite monument, where upon are engraved—in eight different languages, on four giant stones—10 guides, or commandments. Relatively unknown, it is a vital link to the Occult Hierarchy dominating our world. Its origin is shrouded in mystery. In 1979 a well-dress stranger commissioned the project, and requested the building of an edifice to "transmit a message to mankind." He supposedly represented a group who wanted to provide "direction" to humanity. What we now know is the messages deal with four key areas of our lives and living:

1. Establishment of a world government.
2. Population control.
3. Man's relationship to nature.
4. Spirituality.

Agenda 21

The awareness of Agenda 21 is also limited, at best. As a busy culture, we want the quick and easy; however, providing that kind of overview on Agenda 21 may be folly. My intent is to bring you a consciousness to a very complex subject, and encourage you to discover how you, or someone you know, might be victimized by its policies, if you don't dig deeper than the basics!

According to the authors of Agenda 21, the objective is sustainable development, via the integration of economic, social and environmental policies. The desired achievement being a reduction in consumption and social equity, based on environmental impact through control of global land use, education and population control.

I would posture that social equity might indeed become social injustice in the redistribution of wealth, national sovereignty and universal health. I would also suggest you look further into the Proposed Private Partnerships (PPP) wherein special dealings occur between governments and well-chosen corporations allowed tax breaks, grants and other governmental favors such as Eminent Domain... each of which amounts to little more than a government sanctioned monopoly. Further disturbing are the rights and planning of sustainable development policies not intentioned for the well being of the common people.

I would have you look more deeply into the private organizations and government agencies behind Agenda 21, and the government grants driving its process, and to the dimensions of the plan, first introduced to the world in a 1987 report produced by the United Nations World Commission and Development—and authored by the then VP of the World Socialist Party, Gro Harlem Brundtland. I would have you question, "How did something so egregious slip in the front door, and exactly what transpired to give Agenda 21 any ruling authority over our lives?"

Hopefully, as you read the documentation, the language conveying the message that Agenda 21 will require a profound reorientation of all humans, unlike anything the world has ever experienced, too, will disturb you. And, I can only hope you will read deeply enough to see what happens with private property, how governments will be "re-invented" and how individual rights must take a back seat to the needs of the collective.

I can only pray you forget the quick and easy answer you want to hear and see the reality of what a select few will determine as non-sustainable, and what the future will hold for those who dare reveal the underlying conspiracy of a one-world government that serves only the elite.

In light of this expanded awareness, we should still focus on positivity, not negative things, but remain **aware of those who claim to be our protectors when their agenda is to the contrary!** Now, having a foundation as to how as a culture we **descended into a state of sickness and pre-mature death, let's ascend into how we can have radiant health and a vastly extended life spans—if not immortality of our bodies themselves!**

As the author of this discourse, I am fully aware the idea of immortalizing a human body requires a "big stretch" for most people, but I beseech you, "Do not give up on this idea until you read the entire book!"

At the very worst, what is shared in this book can collaterally improve your health—and lengthen your lifespan.

Remember, people lived without electricity to power their homes and businesses for centuries and millennia, yet electricity existed, nevertheless. Now we are learning about pulling electricity from the ethers, via Tesla and other technologies, such as hydrogen fuel cells, without the generating devices and fuels we currently use. The idea of immortality is akin to new energy technologies, something whose time has come and has arrived in the here and now, because of research completed in the past two decades.

Consider the prose by poet, Patrick Sacrementum Regis Steyn, which perfectly sums up the journey of my life—and relates to the blood, sweat and tears I poured into this book and all my other books, for that matter:

New Dimension

All my studies
All my books
People think I'm weird.
They give me strange looks
Month after month
Year after year
Sweating blood
And shedding tears
Seeking the truth
It's out there somewhere.
I've studied so hard
I've even lost my hair
Traveling a path
Mere mortals do not go.
Combating my own demons
Going toe to toe
This battle has continued
What seems a very long time.
Invocations and conjurations
I walk a very thin line.
I've reached a new point
I'm starting to feel the tension
This voice from within my mind
Says I'm guided to a new dimension.

~ Patrick Sacramentum Regis Steyn

So, let this exhilarating journey begin. Well, at least for me… my journey has been such, although certainly with very

1

little support, on my remote path, where very few dare to venture! I have learned when we till the seeds of a fruit tree into the ground, the seeds will germinate under the right conditions, where there is fertility in the soil, enough water to soften the exterior of the seed so the enzyme inside the seed can create a sprout that can root itself into the ground. With the proper care, the tree matures and eventually produces fruit and this fruit will be replicated with fractal perfection. Come to think of it, we are like the seed, for the purposes of this book and in life itself! So let's get things germinating, as it were! I am most hopeful many of my readers will follow the powerful and intoxicating scent to a *new dimension*, where everything is possible, regardless of what you've been told. Like I have often stated... and maybe too often, ha-ha, "The fool did not know it couldn't be done so he went ahead and did it anyway!"

As I've talked to scientists and people with deep esoteric knowledge, they almost universally respond, "Who would want to live forever?" I agree that immortality in the third dimension, which I often refer to as the turd dimension, does not hold a lot of attraction. However, since the process of a body's immortalization actually occurs in the fourth, fifth and even higher dimensions—guess what? Your consciousness correspondingly moves to higher dimensions, to which you may refer to as Heaven. This is the attraction of immortality for me, not because I am afraid to die—since I have done so more than once—but rather living in a body for a long time with the accumulated wisdom I have attained; wisdom that gets pissed away when I keep serially dying.

Serial death is not an efficient use of time on earth... coming and going through the cycle of birth and death.

Please understand... you will join me in undertaking a thorough and wide ranging investigation into immortality. It is this type of cross-disciplinary approach that always leads to the greatest discoveries. As the Greek philosopher Heraclitus stated, "Those who love wisdom must investigate many things."

Before we get started, I want to invite you to become a part of my VIP Reader community, and get a little taste for some of the other writing that, as non-fiction, addresses many of the same issues discussed throughout this book, but in a little less technical manner. You see, I am passionate—ever so passionate about the messages I am intended to deliver— and realize there are readers of every vent out there waiting for me to speak (write) in a tone that both challenges their thinking and inspires the possibilities.

http://www.robertjnewtonauthor.com/vip-readers/

Now! Let's get down to it!

"Vav Vav Lamed," the 43rd Name of God, means making the impossible possible, which means **nothing is impossible**!

לוו

Dr. Robert J. Newton, J.D., N.D.

THE IMMORTALITY PROPHECY

LET THE REVEAL BEGIN!

| Chapter One

Getting Things Done
To a More Radiant Us with a Pathway to Such.

———◇———

When searching for the Holy Grail,
Things rarely come within a hail.
At first we may begin to stutter and flail,
Yet all this certainly is to no avail!
So search for things, far and wide
Therein may the gems so much reside!
Know that nary a thing can ever hide,
So that in truth we may always abide.
But within our very comprehensive search,
Do not ignore those things closest to our perch!
Dr. Robert J. Newton, 10-25-15

———◇———

As an afterthought to the poem above, it should be emphasized, **we should not so much focus on the horizon**

that we miss things that are right in front of our faces!
Often when people try to manifest something new into their
lives, they become so future focused they miss the answers to
their prayers appearing right before them!

I encourage you then, to take heart... since an
immortalized body has already been prophesized for us by
Master Yeshua, Jesus and manifested by:

Kriya Kundalini Yoga Satgurus, including Babaji
Nagaraj, in *The Death of Death,*

Patanjali in The Yoga Sutras, by Thirumoolar in
Thirumunduram,

Hermes Trismegustis in *The Emerald Tablets,*

The Corpus Hermeticum, and in

The "Kaya Kalpa" system of life extension of India,
which is virtually unknown to humanity and even the
people of India, and really even, unto me... in its
complete form.

Additionally, we have Enoch in *The Book of Enoch,*
which was edited out of *The Torah,* ascending into the
heavens, just as Jesus would later.

In our prevailing allopathic medical system you will
receive no such guidance, only a map to your eventual death.
Yes, physicians might extend your life span, but more than
likely this longer life will not be lived with any vigor or
cogent thought processes! Would you not agree, this is not
even a zero sum game, since it would be easier and more
enjoyable to die and move on into a higher dimension, such

as in Heaven, where you do not have to deal with a continually deteriorating body?

Thus, the allopathic medical system and pharmaceutical companies were just excoriated and you might presume we are done with their underhanded ways; unfortunately, such an assumption would be incorrect. In fact our allopathic system of medicine is at the very least partly responsible for our lack of health and longevity; in reality, this system is completely responsible for these things. It is often proclaimed by medical science, we have extended the life spans of people with our "miracle medicines." However, the quality of these longer life spans is high compromised at best. Who wants to live a long life when you feel like shi-ite?

Although this is in contravention to the prevailing medical understanding, everything is energy and not dense matter—and I mean everything—including our human bodies and especially our DNA. Over the last twenty years we have learned from research into our DNA, the real reason why we get sick and why we die. There are "buttons," for lack of a better word, called telomere, found in the last three feet of very long DNA strands in our chromosomes. These telomeres are referred to as strands but the pictures I have seen do not really seem to resemble strands, except when they begin to wear out and unravel. What causes this to happen and why it does will be revealed!

Really, however, all of that is irrelevant and what is more germane is that the telomere located in the chromosomes, are responsible for cell replication. In the process of making

3

copies of new cells, they eventually begin to wear out after 45-50 replications and they either start making imperfect copies of cells or stop all duplication of the cells altogether. It is at this point the chromosomes start to unravel, affected by telomere degeneration. At this point the human body descends into diminished health, conditions of disease, such as cancer and the beginning of the process of aging and death! However, do not despair, as there are ways to counteract these effects!

It is important to always stay positive about things since positive emotions like laughter and smiling are immeasurably better for us than anger, sorrow and stress!

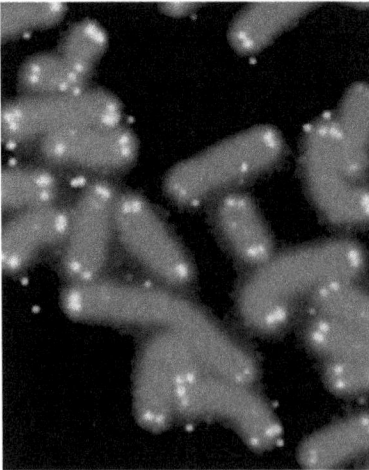

This theme will be apparent throughout this treatise, over and over again! It does us no good to descend into negativity, and may actually cause a lot of harm to your DNA, telomeres and just reflect, too, how our life will "flow" or not. Happy flows— depressed, blows!

FIG #1

Fig. 1, seen above represents chromosomes in red, and the telomere, represented by the yellow dots.

Note: The images in the print version of this book are in greyscale. However, if you want to gain the greatest benefit from referencing them, I encourage you to slip over to my website and request a laminated, color copy of all images in the book.

So does this predicament mean we are doomed to degenerate into bad health and death, as virtually everyone already believes? No! In fact, take heart; it is not inevitable we experience this fate, as it would seem, since there is an enzyme—a "nectar" of sorts—known as telomerase, which in fact can keep the telomere from degenerating or wearing out! We know this from studies that have been completed on rats and mice, which indicate those given telomerase enzyme supplementation have vastly increased health and life spans... three to four times beyond what is considered ordinary. In 2010, a Dana-Farber Cancer Institute study conducted at Harvard University, using telomerase enzyme on rats, revealed not only better overall health, but also a reversal of the aging process in these rats, which were genetically bred to be deficient in telomerase enzyme. Another study with mice at the Spanish National Cancer Center got the same results as the Dana-Farber study... and also cured cancer in the mice.

Now, there has been some concern that telomerase reactivation of telomere leads to the generation of cancer cells. This may be the case when an outside injection of telomerase enzyme into the body goes beyond the optimal level therefore. Yet in neither the Dana-Farber study nor the Spanish Cancer Center Study, was this case. If telomerase enzyme is naturally produced, as the body generates it—

through what will be covered in succeeding chapters herein —as opposed to human intervention of applying such, we should experience a more propitious approach to telomerase enzyme generation. In fact, it would more appear the damaged cells from incorrect cell replication by the telomere might actually be a significant factor in generating cancer cells. So why do the allopathic medical system and pharmaceutical companies not gravitate to and embrace such revolutionary research? Plain and simple...

There is not enough money to be made from the generating telomerase enzyme to cure cancer, improve our health and extend our life spans!

In later chapters, you will find this to be even more understandable!

A connection between our emotions and our thoughts— and even our predominate brainwaves—is revealed through the amounts of telomerase enzyme we naturally produce in our bodies, and subsequently, how our genes and DNA are manifested. Further, could there be an emotional, thought, or brainwave connection with telomere degeneration, as well? There appear to be no studies undertaken on this specific subject, however, the connection between our emotions and thoughts is well established regarding sickness and disease, found in the publications *Science and Health with Key to the Scriptures, A Map to Healing and Your Essential Divinity Through Theta Consciousness, Your Emotions and Your Health,* and *You Can Heal Your Body.* Each is a cutting edge book dealing in depth with this topic.

Another issue that is germane to this discussion is discussed in Dan Winter's documentary, *The Purpose of DNA,* where it is revealed that we get good, or complete cell replication where the telomere are surrounded by strong magnetic fields. Conversely, we get bad or incomplete cell replication in the presence of weak magnetic fields, including the production of cancerous cells, which are damaged or incomplete replications that cause havoc inside of our bodies. Does this not naturally lead us to the question of whether negative emotions, including anger, resentment and sorrow, in fact would create a diminished/lowly charged magnetic field inside our bodies? Let's investigate this!

So while there are no specific studies on the emotional connection to the production of telomerase enzyme and the magnetic fields that affect proper cell division, there is evidence that does reveal a connection between the altered brainwaves of alpha and theta as being progenitors of producing telomerase, which comes from the relaxed properties these brainwaves play in removing stress and negative emotions.

This was clearly revealed in two studies by Dr. Dean Ornish and Dr. Elizabeth Blackburn who put a study group on a vegetarian diet, exercise and regular mediation, which revealed a 10% increase in telomerase enzyme after several months of this regimen in a 2008 study at UCSF in the Prevention Medicine Research Institute. A follow-up five-year study by Ornish and Blackburn also revealed the same results, while the control group show a 3% decrease in the subjects telomere who had not performed the protocols of the study.

Note: After myriad years study of this topic, much understanding and awareness has been gleaned—much remembered, not all precisely cited. It is not the author's intent to fail to adhere to proper writing style, but when a large block of knowledge comes from memory, rather than recent research and/or citation it is not possible to accurately denote the information used. Therefore, throughout the book readers will find respectful references noted; not cited.

A 2016 Harvard University study of blood samples, conducted by Elissa Epel, Jue Lin, et.al., found that genes were expressed differently in people who meditated versus those who did not, in regard to increased cellular metabolism and reduced oxidative stress. This study found meditators produced significantly more telomerase enzyme in immune cells. There was significantly less stress in the meditators and this too has been shown to increase telomerase activity. The implications of this might escape some of the readers of this book, but as you watch the evidence of not having to deteriorate, as will be shared herein, you will see an overwhelming amount of evidence to support, at the very worst, vastly extended and vibrant life spans for us!

There are myriad other studies regarding the body's need for rest published in various sleep journals, which reveal that less than seven hours sleep leads to a degeneration in the telomere and at least seven hours of sleep lead to lengthened telomere.

A brainwave residual effect could also affect the magnetic field component to cell replication, as well, since we know depressed and negative thoughts will prevent the brain or mind from entering the alpha and theta realms of being and consciousness, with corresponding lower energy fields in our bodies. This might reveal the alpha and theta brainwaves responsible for higher magnetic fields in the human body. Does this mean telomerase enzyme is being produced? We know this is essential for proper and continued cell replication.

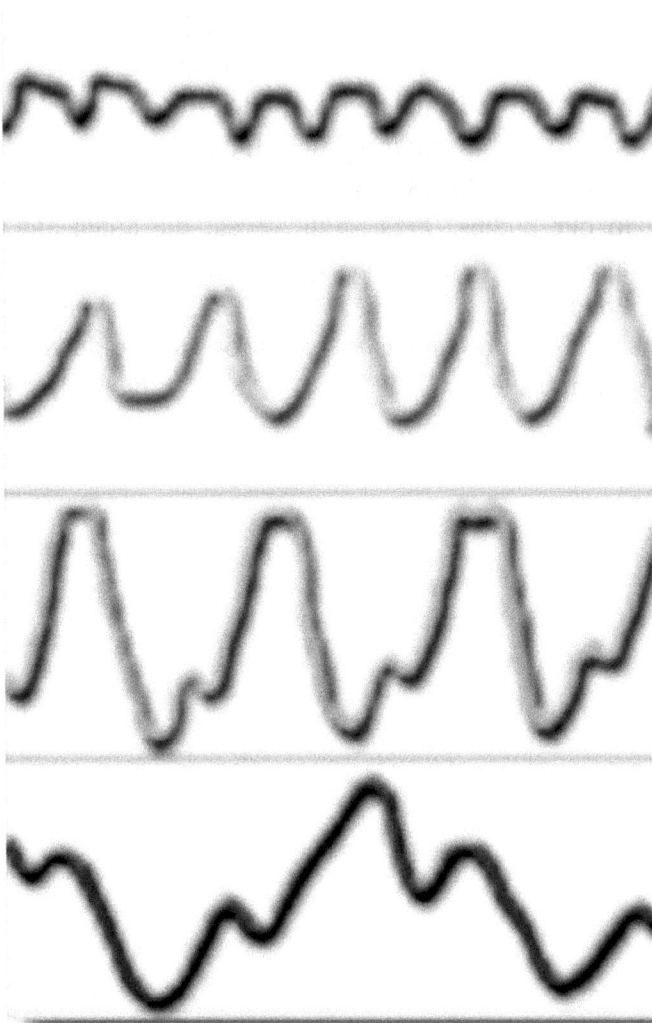

FIG #2: The chart above reveals the four major brainwaves but not the gamma range, which is a highly excited brainwave level sometimes valuable in accomplishing intense tasks.

In the tighter and smaller brainwave in the top of the chart is the **Beta brainwave**, that occurs at about $13-14$ Hertz (Hz), and higher Hz frequencies, where there is little deep focusing or relaxation of the human mind and body and this is what some people call "the Monkey Mind," because it is a very scattered and distracted state of consciousness.

At the second brainwave from the top, we find **Alpha**, in the range of 7-13 or 14 Hz. where more concentration and less body stress are encountered and wherein telomerase enzyme can be produced.

Notice how this brainwave is larger in height and there is more space between the waves, which we find even more exaggerated in the brainwave at third from the top, which is denoted as Theta. Everything in Alpha is more pronounced in Theta as are the benefits commensurate there from; Theta is denoted in the 4-7 Hz range.

Finally, at the bottom, we have Delta, which shows us a very relaxed wave, associated with sleep and yet it is possible with practice, for wakeful meditation to occur in Delta, which conveys the highest levels of higher consciousness and stress relief and telomerase activity. Delta occurs at 4 Hz. and below.

The alpha and especially theta and upper delta brainwaves are what stimulate telomerase enzyme—the rejuvenating substance for our telomere and what allow accurate cell replication. There seem to be no studies on magnetic fields and brainwave correlation, **but we know the magnetic properties of negative ions in fact will stimulate**

11

alpha and theta brainwaves. So from this awareness it is plausible to infer the connection between these two concepts.

All this information deals with epigenetics, meaning how our thoughts and emotions mutate or affect things inside and outside our bodies. This subject is discussed in Deepak Chopra's *Super Genes* and Bruce Lipton's *The Biology of Belief*. Yet what is revealed in this book, as we attempt to go deeper, is to literally unveil the practices and protocols that allow us to be the "master of our fate." This means our DNA and genes are not "set in stone" and are very mutable and controllable, irrespective of what you might have been told and what sadly is universally believed.

So, it would not seem farfetched to proclaim…

our emotions and thoughts and our brainwave status affect our telomere, chromosomes and DNA… because the evidence supports such.

These things just listed would be considered epigenetic factors that modify DNA and the things related thereto. So to repeat again, there is definitely a **connection between our dominant brain waves and the production of telomerase enzyme!** This will be discussed in depth in succeeding chapters, beginning in Chapter Two.

There are supplements, herbs, vitamins, etc. that will stimulate telomerase enzyme, and start us off in the right direction. One supplement is Product 'B' and another is TA 65. Vitamins A, B12, C, D6, E and K2 also stimulate the enzyme. The minerals Zinc and Magnesium likewise stimulate telomerase enzyme. Then we have a long list of herbs, which also stimulate the telomerase enzyme:

Haematococcus pluvialis (Astaxanthin)	Silymarin
	Purslane
Turmeric	Ginkgo biloba

We also have fermented foods like Miso, Sauerkraut and Kombucha mushrooms that stimulate telomerase, as well. The Telomerase enzyme is also stimulated by Omega 3 Fatty Acids found in raw Flaxseed oil, Krill oil, Salmon, Sardines, and Mackerel; Co-enzyme Q10, Epitalon, Maltese Mushrooms and Probiotics, such L Acidophilus, L Bifidus, L Racemosa, Lactobacillus plantarum, L salivarius, and the ageLOC® Youth product.

Another supplement I must mention is Human Growth Hormone (HGH), chemically known as somatotropin, and precursors thereof. Other than the Tulsi Basil, which has a strong relaxing effect on a human mind and body (and please keep in mind how we just considered how stress reduction is a catalyst to creating telomerase), the studies re HGH are really mind blowing as to its beneficial effect regarding life extension. Dr. Richard Marsh, renowned neurosurgeon, states there are many studies that indicate HGH deficiency is directly related to poor health, early onset degenerative disease and premature death (and from what I have learned, **all death is premature—yes—all death is premature**)!

A Russian doctor, Dillman, discovered more than two decades ago that diminishing hormones in the body lead to its degeneration. He believed that hormone supplementation could slow down the aging process and even reverse it. the bad news is that HGH starts to diminish around twenty-five to thirty years old in a human. My strong intuition tells me this denegation of the telomeres and lessening HGH is really related to negative emotions and stress.

Several researchers and physicians have shared their findings in the significance of HGH in increased longevity. Franco Salamon, in London England, found HGH increased body muscle mass 10% while it reduced fat by 7% and led to significant increase in bone mass; this is supported as well by Dr. Ed Dorman, who has administered natural HGH to thousands of patients. Dr. Edmund Chein, who authored, *Age Reversal,* and founded The Palm springs Life Extension Institute, found a 75% increase in male sexual functions, 88% increase in muscle mass, 72 % fat loss, 81% increase in exercise tolerance and 83% increase in exercise endurance when people were given HGH, daily. Dr. Richard Marsh, Life Extension expert states, "Increasing level of HGH in an older person is like giving water to someone dying of thirst." Dr. Daniel Rudman, Director of Geriatric Medicine at Chicago Medical School, University of Health Sciences relayed in *The New England Journal of Medicine,* giving daily injections of HGH to people helped them to reduce their fat levels by 14%, increase lean muscle mass by 9%, improve their skin tone and improve sexual drive. [1]

---

[1]

kadenchiropractic.com/clients/2348/documents/**Fountain__of_You**th_Handout.pdf

Now here comes the exciting part because instead of using HGH injections, Dr. Dorman, mentioned above, found at The American College for Advancement of Medicine, that HGH can be created through precursor of secretagogue (a substance that promotes secretion) compounds taken orally through stacked amino acids, namely, glycine, glutamine and arginine. We further known the brain can secrete HGH during the sleep state of delta brainwaves. Norman Shealy discovered the Pituitary gland is stimulated by a 7.8-Hertz photic stimulus, which produces HGH in the human body!

So let's get back to the brainwaves of alpha, theta and delta because they not only stimulate telomerase, they also stimulate HGH, as Dr. Vincent C. Giampapa, ex-president of The American Board of Anti-Aging Medicine, discovered. Related to this, research psychologist, Ernest Rossi, found that when we visualize our ideal self/image, we release neuropeptides that allow us to create an entire new body in eleven months.

There is another aging factor and that is the Hydroxyl radical, a type of oxidative stress, which damages our DNA including our chromosomes and telomere. This can be easily be remediated by infusing more Hydrogen into the human body. This can be done through hydrogen pills and water filters which we will discuss in chapter 10. Both hydrogen and Vitamin C are antioxidants, which can penetrate the mitochondria and thus negate the effects of radicals, even though hydrogen is not normally considered an antioxidant.

We will also discover many more amazing things about Hydrogen in chapters six and ten, as well as many other cutting edge things in chapter two and beyond.

What we are capable of is most amazing.

It is time to remove the veiled knowledge that has been hidden from the citizens of planet Earth. There are things much more potent, and which more powerfully generate telomerase enzyme and many more beneficial things—like altered brainwaves in the alpha, theta, delta and gamma range—with commensurately increased psychic abilities and enhanced creativity and problem solving. So let's continue with that. You could find all of this delicious as well as duh-licious!

| CHAPTER TWO

GOING A LOT DEEPER WITH MORE TO CHEW WHAT HAPPENS ON THE ATOMIC LEVEL OF CREATION AND HOW DO WE REPROGRAM OUR MINDS INTO A STATE OF IMPROVED HEALTH AND IMMORTALITY?

When you need to go so very deep,
You'll never find such following sheep,
So go hew and cut your own trail,
For thereon will you most likely prevail!
Dr. Robert J. Newton 10-26-15

WE ARE ABOUT to go "so very deep" in blazing our own trails, but all of this is logical and intuitive and can be demonstrated if we allow it be so! Be of great courage and give your mind permission to be pliable and adaptive; something the subconscious or unconscious mind tends to prevent us from doing. As humans, we are normally much more comfortable with "business as usual" or doing things in the manner to which our minds are accustomed.

> *You owe it to yourself to be aware of the proclivity of a brain operating system that would rather remain the same… rather than change!*

Now we know there are more things than telomere shortening, which lead to sickness and aging, including glycation, which according to various medical dictionaries is a nonenzymatic covalent bonding of a sugar molecule to another molecule, especially a protein. We find also… oxidative stress, water with high levels of deuterium and stressful factors encountered in living life on planet Earth, that negatively affect our telomere in our chromosomes. In the case of both glycation and oxidative stress, glucose sugar binds to DNA, proteins and lipids and causes cell degeneration. These things could be related to the nucleus of a cell no longer being able to communicate with the mitochondria, wherein degeneration of the body begins. Additionally, hydroxyl radicals, mentioned at the end of Chapter One, are part of oxidative stress.

Further, there is no evidence to contradict how general life stress has been shown to create sickness and disease, yet much to support such, including Louise L. Hay's groundbreaking book, *You Can Heal Your Body* and in Emrika Padus' *Your Emotions and Your Health*. Water with high levels of Hydrogen, such as Hydrogen Peroxide (H_2O_2) and H_3O_2 (EZ-water) will eliminate and/or lower the levels of deuterium in water and also counteract hydroxyl radicals.

Even anti-depressants will not negate the effects of stress since they really do not eliminate the cause of stress, only put the body in a tranquilized state but not the brain/mind that is the originator of a depressed or stressed mind. Now we can reprogram our minds to get to the causative factors of disease and death, and removing them from our minds. Please refer to *A Map to Healing and Your Essential Divinity Through Theta Consciousness,* by Dr. Robert J. Newton and *Miracles, Momentum and Manifestation*, by Anna Weber, et al.

The telomerase enzyme does not apparently counteract these things, but we could reprogram the human mind to through Neuro Linguistic Programing (NLP), Silva Mind Control and Theta Consciousness Reprogramming, as per *A Map to Healing and Your Essential Divinity Through Theta Consciousness*. These protocols are based on brain science and should not be lightly considered as arbitrary notions. We can do the same thing to the telomere, to **reprogram the mind for all of these things and negate the processes of degeneration!** Please keep in mind, atoms do not degenerate nor should the cells, which are comprised of these atoms! This was covered in depth by Dr. Francoise Tibika, at the Science and Non Duality Conference 2015 in San Jose, California in her presentation, *On Atoms and Perception.*

In fact, we could say, that the processes of degeneration have been forced and foisted upon us through incessant propaganda/public relations by those who would rather we are sick and slowly degenerate. Remember, a few people and their corporations make obscene profits from all of this... from our misfortune! In the fields of public relations and propaganda, we know most people will believe something whether it is true or not, if it is repeated enough times. What we perceive and feel is what the brain-computer will file in our brain and then, without fail, it will replicate such files as events in our lives.

> *The government, religions, the allopathic medical establishment, pharmaceutical companies and corporations all know this and depend on human nature to influence us, to program us to perceive things in their desired manner, and virtually always contrary to our best interests!*

A good example of this concept is Darwin's "Theory of Evolution," as reported in "The American Press," many years ago. When Darwin first released his theory, it was widely discredited and scoffed at by his peers... other scientists. After a massive public relations campaign, funded by the controllers of our planet, as was mentioned in the prologue, a reversal of opinion occurred—and all of a sudden there was a building of support for his theory, and a theory only with very little substantive scientific backing therefore!

To theorize humans came from apes, when there is no proof of such, other than similarities between apes and Cro-Magnon man and Neanderthal peoples as an assumption, is rather astonishing. Why could not apes have come from humans? Certainly there are shared genetic markers, yet you cannot assume from this they are related. At the most, you can only assume they are similar!

I have seen many different scenarios of creation and none of them talk about humans emerging from apes, except that of Darwin. Additionally, Michael A. Cremo, who provided scientific evidence that challenged standard views on human evolution in his books, including *Forbidden Archaeology,* revealed the outright flaws in Darwin's "theory," based on the timeline for creation as being short and disputed by 55-million-year evidence of humans and artifacts discovered in a mine at Tuolumne, Table Mountain, in California.

Even in his twelve books, including *When Time Began,* Zecharia Sitchin, revealed in his research, the genetically modified human DNA, mixed with that of the Annunaki, who were the main gods of the Sumerian civilization, believed to have come to Earth from the planet Nibiru. Even today, this testing and mixing of different DNA is being done in the U.S. government Defense Advanced Research Projects Agency (DARPA) program. There may have been a mixing of human DNA and Anunaki DNA, since there are common DNA markers, yet not enough to proclaim as Sitchin asserted.

It appears there may have been deliberate mixing of human and animal DNA, if the things in Greek mythology in fact are a reality of sorts (Centaurs, Pegasus, Bacchus, Unicorns et al.), and if you think about it, how else would these creatures be described unless they actually existed. **It has likewise been hypothesized the Anunaki genetically modified the people of Earth,** which differs greatly from Darwin's humans evolving from apes. So Darwin can RIP or in pieces!

Another even better example of manipulating humans through propaganda is attributing global warming to man-made carbon emissions on our planet. Now, undeniably there are substantial man made carbon emissions, however, there are so many factors involved with temperature increase—including the angle of Earth on its axis vis-à-vis the Sun—and the amount of fuel the Sun has with which to combust. It just so happens there is the cloud of hydrogen from an exploded star, which our Sun is transiting through—and more hydrogen equals more fuel for more combustion and the resulting heat therefrom! At the very worst, these would be significant co-factors causing global warming, yet one must wonder why these are never a part of the "global warming" discussion. Furthermore, why are the substantial carbon emissions from termites not factored into the global warming calculations?

If this topic piques your interest, you may read a more complete explanation on my blog post, *Removing the Shackles* (http://bit.ly/RemovingShackles). You should also be aware that every time the Earth has a large increase in the temperature, our planet has always gone into an Ice Age, the last one occurring about ten thousand years ago! So while we are being bombarded with public relations and propagandized into believing the Earth will get too hot, what we really have in our future is an impending Ice Age on the horizon! So much for the idiotic ranting of the U.N., railing against global warming! All of these disingenuous messages are to get us to support a U.N. carbon tax from a people already being taxed into poverty, namely, us, the Earth's inhabitants. Global warming was debunked in 1990, in Dr. Eben Browning's documentary, *Climate and the Affairs of Man* as well as in 2016 in Michael Hanley's, *Dark Winter*.

We could add to the growing list of deceit, the propaganda campaign to convince us massive species "die off." In reality, such species being eliminated are rarely if ever listed; all we get is a general claim the purging occurs, with no quantification of the numbers of animals being decimated!

Anyway, lest we get carried to far with these asides, let's get back to the atomic level of creation, where we see the nine geometric forms of creation replicating themselves over and over again in atoms—and we see certain wave patterns doing the same, which represent the result of cymatic forces or vibrations from the "primal sound" of Aum/Om and "The Intelligent Cosmic Vibration," as noted in the *Bhagavad Gita*, page 369, of the Paramahansa Yogananda translation. These atomic and wave form perfections are clearly revealed in Valery P. Kondratov's, *Geometry of a Uniform Field*. Since we have "hard evidence" of these things from pictures via helium ion microscopes, the perfection of these indestructible atoms and the cells resulting there from, is clearly revealed to us. Furthermore, no degenerating factor related to atoms, any imperfection, to wit, has been discovered there about. Do you not question that with atoms as their only component, why cells degenerate?

We certainly could initialize the process of cell deterioration through human thoughts and emotions, of the negative variety found in anger, stress, depression, etc.

Robert J. Newton

Thoughts of ultimate deterioration have been planted in us incessantly—in our so-called medical science—and the propaganda that supports such. Hence, this reality only reinforces the importance of us taking control of the information in our minds! This action is not a onetime event, rather it is akin to daily sessions of meditation and cancelling the incessant propaganda stream trying to manipulate and guide our thoughts to the lowest level rather than the realms of the Divine that are our deific inheritance and right to possess.

In Fig. 3 as follows, platinum crystals photographed by Dr. Erwin Mueller, circa 1953, show the nine geometric forms of creation, from Valery P. Kondratov's *Geometry of a Uniform Field*.

Viewing FIG #3 returns us to the importance of re-programming our human brain-computer, to remove therefrom incorrect and imperfect thoughts and information and replace our thoughts with the perfection that has been staring us in the face while all this time we were consciously unaware! The Platinum crystal matrix goes a long way to demonstrate the perfect of creation, as per the 7th Name of God, Aleph Kaf Aleph.

Positive mind reprogramming was mentioned earlier and an easy way to achieve it is through engaging in **Neuro Linguistic Programming (NLP) "Swishing."** The information can be more thoroughly explored in one of my previous publications, *Pathways to God: Experiencing the Energies of the Living God in Your Everyday Life*. This mind programming technique is quick and effective. My "Theta Consciousness Reprogramming and Healing" technique is explained in detail in Chapter Four of *A Map to Healing and Your Essential Divinity Through Theta Consciousness: Physics of the Immortal "Light Body" and the Creator's Template of Perfection and Abundance for His People*. This is undoubtedly one of the most comprehensive ways to reprogram the human mind and to create a healing state within the human body!

Do we need these techniques or processes to enter a state of improved health and longevity? Most likely and they definitely can bring the desired results!

Fig. 4 is a diagram and explanation of NLP "Swishing" technique. Imagine, looking at the images below, a situation you want to change in your mind, as being much like a dead tree—representing what we don't want in life.

The swishing process involves looking at the "unwanted" in our lives, such as a dead tree, and to then imagine a healthy tree that is "installed" and pictured in our minds. To install the healthy tree (picture) in your mind, you move a small image of the new (wanted) healthy tree picture from the lower left corner of the picture into the area occupied by the dead tree, which is the swishing, enlarging it as you expand it to the upper right hand corner. Ultimately, the old picture fades away and the new picture "program" replaces the old one—as your mind swishes or merges the new picture of the healthy tree over the top of the dead tree. This swishing process works with health issues, business, prosperity… or any topic where you seek deeper understanding or change.

FIG #4

There is another simple, spur of the moment mind programming and/or reprogramming technique from **Silva Mind Control**, pioneered by **Jose Silva**. It involves repeating two words, **"Cancel, cancel,"** whenever we hear something that is contrary to our best interests. Some people prefer to use, **"Cancel, cancel, clear,** instead of just "Cancel, cancel." So if someone tells us, "Death and taxes are inevitable," and if we sincerely desire is to have an immortalized body of light, sans the obligation of paying taxes, we would say aloud, "Cancel, cancel," and expect the untruths to be cancelled and not encoded into our computer-brain. Some people using this technique say,

This "Cancel, cancel," routine can be part of the gate keeper mentality to our brains; with this established, let us move forward and examine powerful ways to create more telomerase enzymes so we can circumvent degenerated health and a deteriorating body. The following things have been revealed to create telomerase enzyme: general meditation, Qui Gong, Sudarshan Kriya, Tai Chi, Kriya Kundalini Pranayam(a) (a breathing meditation), Samadhi, the feeling of Love (including kissing, sexual union and more), *The Gayatri Mantra, The Mahamrityunjaya Mantra, The Aum Mantra,* "The 72 Names of God," from Exodus 14, vs. 19-21 in *The Torah,* being under or near a pyramid structure, structured water (H_3O_2 EZ-water), inheriting DNA that produces more telomerase enzyme, leyline vortexes, Yoga Asanas (stretching), regular stretching, dancing, singing, laughing, comedy—and hallucinogenic substances like Ayahuasca and Psilocybin, and Ormus/monatomic Gold.

Pyramids and leyline vortexes are covered in Chapter Seven and Ayahuasca and Psilocybin Mushrooms in Chapter Eight. Delving into each individually, in the Shamatha Project study it was discovered that even just general mediation, in an intensive manner for three months, produces a thirty percent increase in the secretion of telomerase enzyme. Another study by the Northern Arizona University, in 2013, revealed theta brainwaves, in the 4-7 Hertz range, were produced in deep meditation, with experienced meditators. This suggests if we produce alpha and theta brainwaves, telomerase is produced in the body because that is what is produced in the brain tomography during deep meditation.

Such deep states of meditation are revealed in the practitioners of Qui Gong, the Tai Chi "Standing Meditation," Kundalini Yoga and Kriya Kundalini Pranayam(a). Fig. 5 is a brain map/brain tomography showing the theta brainwaves produced during Kundalini Yoga. We find the same brainwaves in the Tai Chi "Standing Meditation" and Kriya Kundalini Pranayam.

Another study with meditators, conducted by the Dalai Lama and Cutler, in 2009,[2] revealed decreased psychological distress and a significant promotion of well being for the study participants. In another study by Dr. Elissa Epel,[3] et al.—where meditators meditated for six hours a day for three months—revealed reduced cortisol and neuroticism in the participants and increased production of telomerase enzyme; this would apply, likewise to the Dalai Lama and Cutler study. This second study also discovered more cell vitality in the meditators such as would be revealed in an MMR cell measurement that measure cell energy/vitality. The evidence points to a direct correlation between the elimination of stress and the production of telomerase enzyme, distilled as such:

---

[2] med.stanford.edu/scopeblog/sdarticle.pd

[3] http://sanfrancisco.cbslocal.com/2014/10/18/ucsf-study-links-soda-to-premature-aging-disease-early-death/

meditation = improved psychological outlook= increased telomerase enzyme = increased health/longevity!

Fig. 5 reveals theta brainwaves produced in a practitioner of Kundalini Yoga, most within the theta brainwave range of 4-7 Hertz (Hz) and in the Alpha range, 7-13 Hz.

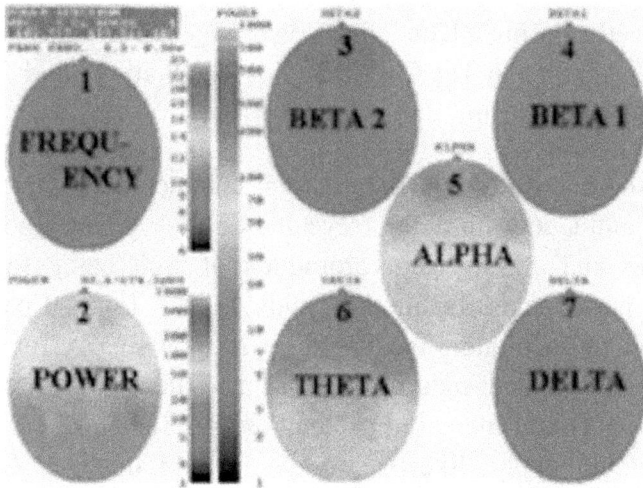

FIG #5 shows the effect of Kundalini Yoga meditation producing alpha, theta and delta brainwaves on participants in a study. Notice that at the top of the frame, the EEG starts in beta and progressively transition into alpha, then theta and eventually... delta. Getting to delta would manifest only for advanced practitioners of these disciplines.

I also suggest you study a published article found on the website, Complimentary Therapies in Clinical Practice, which accumulates fifteen studies in Yoga entitled, *The Effects of*

Yoga on Brainwaves and Structural Integration by Radhika Desai, Anisha Taylor and Tani Bhatt. It will be an aid in your understanding the consistent pattern of alpha and theta waves experienced during Kundalini Yoga meditation and Pranayam. A picture of brainwaves through brain tomography is worth at least a thousand words and fifteen studies validating each other are of commensurate value as well. The downloadable PDF of this article can be purchased at: http://www.ctcpjournal.com/article/S1744-3881(15)00011-0/fulltext

There is another study conducted by Jeffrey A. Dusak at Harvard Medical School in 2008—using MTT cell analysis—that measured the cell metabolic activity/vitality completed on practitioners of Kundalini Yoga over the period of twenty days.[4] At the end of these twenty days, there was an average increase of 967% in cellular energy levels—as revealed by the MTT assay. Does this indicate a direct connection between telomerase enzymes in Kundalini Yoga practitioners? Really, no… not necessarily, but it does show a vast energy infusion into body cells that could revitalize the telomere in the chromosomes in the DNA as well or better than telomerase enzyme.

This would correlate with the benefits associated with strong magnetic fields aiding in the process of cell division. In "Effects of 60Hz AC Magnetic Fields on Gene Expression

---

[4] http://www.allinahealth.org/Penny-George-Institute-for-Health-and-Healing/Research/

Following Exposure Over Multiple Cell Replications,"[5] by David R. Binninger and Vichate Ungvichian, which revealed increased cell division in 60 Hz. magnetic fields. Adam Lacy-Hulbert, et al., in "Biological Responses to Electromagnetic Fields,"[6] discovered 60 Hz. magnetic fields increased the proliferation of human cells. Of foremost interest—it just so happens—Kriya Kundalini Pranayam and the Tai Chi "Standing Meditation" just so happen to significantly increase the electromagnetic/Prana/Chi. So this would help to direct our efforts to keep our cells healthy and replicating themselves indefinitely.

This increased energy might also create an impetus to create telomerase enzyme. This increase in cell energy is most likely the result of Chi from Taoism and Prana in Kundalini Yoga. This Prana is described as Agna (light) and Yagna (fire) on page 369 of the Paramahansa Yogananda translation of *The Bhagavad Gita,* a revered Hindu and Yogic text. This Prana/Chi energy comes from three known sources, aside from the *Bhagavad Gita*:

1. Galactic center of the Milky Way Galaxy,

2. Sun, and

3. Atomic field (the vast field of atoms which surrounds us and from which we are comprised).

The Immortality Prophecy

We must embrace how the Sun would be a central factor in all of this, as would the electromagnetic energy and scalar waves that emanate from the Sun and the center of the Milky Way Galaxy. Some scalar researchers consider scalar waves separate from electromagnetic waves; however, T. Galen Hieronymus, one of the earliest scalar wave researchers, states scalar waves can become electromagnetic waves and vice versa. So are they the same or different? The answer to this may be a semantic or diagrammatic trap, but we do not have to have an answer to this question to draw a conclusion.

We do know, however, energy from the Sun provides 48.115 megawatts—by some estimates and 400 trillion watts of energy by other measurements—and this accessible energy comes to our planet, continually, each second of the day. This is more than enough energy to supply Earth's energy needs... primarily generated by the burning of coal, gasoline, natural gas, nuclear power, and readily available for our use, as Nikola Tesla demonstrated in a conclusive test at the Wycliffe Tower. For the purpose of immortalizing our human bodies, we likewise need to harness the Sun's energy, whether it be electrical or scalar in form.

What we also have come to know is there is a connection between Kundalini Yoga and Kriya Kundalini Pranayam breathing and bringing more Agna (light) and Yagna (fire) into the human body via the process and referred to in *The Bhagavad Gita,* page 369 of the Paramahansa Yogananda translation and referred to as "The Intelligent Cosmic Vibration." This energy or vibration is comprised of the fire and light electromagnetic energy, and cymatic or vibrational

33

forces of Aum, the Sanskrit primal sound of creation. It could also be more than a random occurrence that Nikola Tesla said the numbers 3, 6, and 9 are not only the keys to the Universe, but understanding the energy therein. We know Tesla was deeply involved with scalar technology, although he called it something else; I take you deeper into these numbers in Chapter Four, but at this point in time let it just be said that understanding the germ atria (number(s)) behind all letters, words, and concepts), gives us great insight into things not otherwise discernable.

And... while mentioning Yagna (fire), it is important to point out that some practitioners of Qui Gong can cause newspaper to combust, just using the focused energy from their hands. You can easily find videos to support the practice on the Internet. It is from information such as this and other readily available evidence we are able to gain previously unknown insights into some of life's "mysteries" and ascertain whether Prana/Chi are active forces in the Universe. It is from a constant search to collect shards of evidence that a larger picture of things becomes more apparent as per the poem below:

'Those who search far and wide,
Will more likely in truth abide.
By undertaking a thorough search,
We will never be besmirched.
Dr. Robert J. Newton, 10-27-15

THERE APPEARS TO be a direct relationship between the alpha and even more importantly, theta brainwaves, and the stimulation of telomerase enzyme. This is a synchronicity rather than random-ness, and it is propitious and more so, fantastic for us, the things previously listed produce these brainwaves. We can rest assured because the technology available as brain tomography through EEG brain scans provides supporting evidence.

In the realm of sexuality, we have theta brainwaves being produced during sexual orgasm; yes the same sexual orgasm that many sources reference as dirty; debased but still somehow necessary and enjoyable.

More than necessary, these wonderful orgasms can be life extending as well as highly enjoyable when the theta brainwave factor is added into our immortality equation, when you understand how to pull Kundalini/Prana/Chi/life force energy from the root chakra up into the crown chakra. A picture of these chakras is provided deeper into this book. How this done is explained in Mantak Chia's book mentioned later in this chapter! This is displayed in FIG #6.

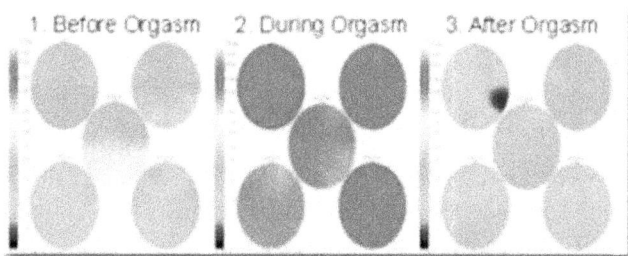

1. Before Orgasm   2. During Orgasm   3. After Orgasm

Before orgasm, *high alpha shows good relaxation.*

During orgasm *there is a huge increase in amplitude of all major frequencies indicating an arousal of the Kundalini energy. All the chakras are activated and the energy is reaching the brain and producing theta brainwaves.*

Immediately following orgasm, *the brain shuts down the feelings, and the energy takes a downward course toward the genitals. All the brain maps show averaged activity over 30 seconds; there also will be remaining theta brainwaves and dips into upper delta waves. If a male becomes a master of delaying or preventing the release of his semen, he can greatly extend the benefit of the normal 39-second duration of theta brainwaves into multi-minutes to even an hour or more!*

The proof is in the pictures, which literally shows the theta brainwaves created during a sexual orgasm and a dip into delta, and also aid in stimulating telomerase enzyme in the human body. I posture, "Can there be anything perceived as ungodly unless being done in a sexually abusive manner?" Likewise, can there really be anything not divine about kissing? It might be time to send these ideas back to the Puritans, Calvinists, or others who support a Brahmacharya or life style of celibacy, from back from whence they came!

In a counterpoint to sexual activity, Babaji Nagaraj in *The Death of Death,* Lord Krishna in *The Bhagavad Gita* and Paramahansa Yogananda in his writings, explain that Brahmacharya, is necessary to achieve an immortalized body and union with God. Yet Stephen Thomas Chiang in *The Tao of Sexuality: The Book of Infinite Wisdom* and Mantak Chia in *Taoist Secrets of Love: Cultivating Male Sexual Energy* share

36

how sexuality is a portal to immortalizing the human body. Both of these books are spiritual sexuality approaches to immortality; it is possible to view the Indian Tantric approach in the same vein, where delaying or preventing male ejaculation leads to state of spiritual ecstasy and the alpha, theta, and upper delta brainwaves that can be produced.

The Taoist Master, Mantak Chia, is quite adamant that advanced sexuality is a direct portal to immortality. The Taoist and Tantric approach to orgasm is for the male to withhold the release of semen during ejaculation. It is widely believed by Taoists and those schooled in Tantrism, yet never proven by any measurements, the releasing of semen physically depletes the male human body, because the life force energies of Chi and Prana are lost in that release of fluids!

What I now propose: since there are trillions of watts of energy emanating from the Sun, and a constant field of energy being released in the atomic field—a piezoelectric electrical or pranic energy from individual and aggregated atoms—there is little to no energy depleted in the male body after ejaculation and even if there is, such energy is quickly replaced. In fact, we must also integrate other aspects: altered brainwaves produced during sexual orgasm, the beneficial effects of the alpha and theta brainwaves in creating a state of spiritual elevation, entering higher dimensions of experience and functioning, concomitant with the production with more telomerase enzyme being produced in our bodies— each of which leads to improved health, extended life spans and possibly... immortality.

In light of myriad concepts, which speak a different message, it becomes increasingly difficult to fathom how the male ejaculation could really deplete a male body and it easier to conclude an elevated state of bodily energy is ultimately produced... providing more benefit than detriment. Very possibly, one could conclude how both the chastity/Brahmacharya and Taoist/Tantric approaches are valid. Is it really necessary to have an either/or dichotomy?

There is no desire to create unnecessary conflict, but it would also seem wise to pursue anything that is going to create the alpha and theta brainwaves, which will stimulate the immortality enzyme, telomerase human growth hormone (HGH)!

What you read now is deemed so important it gets its own paragraph! An **intense orgasm** puts the body and mind in a state of **deep relaxation;** it is this very deep relaxation that manifests the alpha and theta brainwaves. It is also this very relaxation that allows more Prana/Chi/God life force to course through the body, which means more Agna and Yagna occupies our bodily space and creates more of a light body or Merkabah. These statements can be easily correlated with and verified by the Tai Chi Chuan 'Standing Meditation" that is covered a little later in this chapter.

The more relaxing things we do in this or any other meditation, the more we will feel heat and tingling in our hands, medulla oblongata and spinal column, manifested as life force energy, Prana, or Chi. This tingling and heat are biofeedback, or markers, indicating to us the Prana/Chi/life force are more accumulated in our bodies. Further, we should not forget this relaxed state of body and consciousness stimulates the telomerase enzyme, and for sure we need it to maintain our telomeres to improve our, health, life span and our continued presence on Earth.

If you have followed my line of reasoning, you will see what was revealed regarding the stimulation of the telomerase enzymes, we have both the functions of theta brainwaves, a mental/higher dimension factor, and the Prana/Chi, a life sustaining/cosmic energy factor of light and fire. In Kundalini Yoga are many breathing protocols used for life force energy stimulation. In Kriya Kundalini Yoga, as revealed most recently by Babaji Nagaraj to Lahiri Mahasaya and Yogi Ramaiah, considered as Babaji's designated scribes and teachers, there exist the same breathing protocols of Kundalini Yoga—and even more. The true gem that Kriya Kundalini Yoga has in the Kriya Kundalini Pranayam breathing meditation, which is an 8-0-16-0 breathing protocol, is what transpires when the length of the exhaled breath is retained twice as long as the inhalation.

The ultimate power lies in the ability to take dedicated, seasoned practitioners into a breathless state of Samadhi, in which deep theta and upper delta brainwaves are produced, due to the deep state of relaxation, there from.

There are also seven meditation techniques from Kriya Kundalini Yoga, known as Kriya Dhyana, which is a series of meditation techniques to learn the scientific art of mastering the mind—a mental concentration—and something related thereto, Kriya Dharana—a level of concentration found in the sixth stages of Kriya Kundalini Yoga Dhyana and Dharana. These are very powerful designated meditations that allow us to control the human mind and create a state of focused attention.

Now, as much as I would like to reveal the specifics of the Kriya Kundalini Pranayam breath, which involves exhaling twice as long as the breath inhalation, it is better taught in a class setting as there are many nuances to the Kriya Kundalini Yoga Pranayam breath that require personal instruction.

Another reason it is not wise to learn this technique without a seasoned instructor is some people will have Kundalini awakenings, dimension shifting energy infusions into their bodies, that can be highly disorienting. These statements are made from personal experience and not just remote theory or hearsay. This disorientation is well chronicled in Gopi Krishna's book, *Kundalini for the New Age*. It was also discussed by Dr. Paul Foster Case, of The Golden Dawn Order of Rosicrucians and head of The Builders of the Adytum (BOTA) whereby he admitted that practicing Kriya Kundalini Pranayam was the worst thing he ever did in life, because his experience was so disorienting, and realized he could have very much used the guidance of a teacher for the practice.

Very few people will not be disoriented in this situation; the confusion comes from intense energy dynamics from an immediate shift into the fifth and six dimensions. So

Pranayam does not need to be disorienting; you just need a very experienced teacher or practitioner thereof. You can learn the Kriya Kundalini Yoga Pranayam breath from me by connecting through my website which is listed in the back of the book under resources. In this Kriya Kundalini Yoga Pranayam you learn to enter the theta brainwave status as well as infuse your body with Agna (light) and Yagna (fire), and experience the increased cellular energy levels that are rejuvenating factors of the telomere strands and the entire body in general!

Next, let's address what clinical studies have revealed about the benefits of Kriya Kundalini Pranayam. A study conducted in April 2013, by Su Qu, Solveig Mjelstad Olafsrud, Leonardo A. Meza, Fahri Saatcioglu and Srinivas Mummidi, [7]revealed an effect on the genes (gene expression) from the practice of Pranayam(a), indicating cells can be modified or better expressed/manifested in a stimulation of telomerase enzyme.

Another study by Anne E. Holland, Catherine J. Hill, Alice Y. Jones, and Christine E. MacDonald showed a twenty percent reduction in both stress and asthma symptoms, from the practice of Pranayam(a).[8] The relaxation achieved will then create an environment where more telomerase enzyme is produced in the human body. I hope you are beginning to see continuing evidence that stacks up in favor of the strong value

---

[7] http://www.ncbi.nlm.nih.gov/pmc/articles/PMC3629142/

[8]http://www.epistemonikos.org/documents/c8ae05897415e0a22df1271e8b45c5dfb832ac2c/

of Pranayam. This is just a cursory listing of the studies showing stress reduction, asthma relief, and a corresponding beneficial effect on the autonomic nervous system.

So adding to the cache of Pranayam(a) is the insight of Paramahansa Yogananda. In one of his books, *God Talked with Arjuna: The Bhagavad Gita and Kriya Yoga,* he shares a belief that Kriya Yoga was given to the first man on Earth, Manu, according to *The Vedas.* Further described in verses 4.29, 2.29, and 2.49-2.51 from the very ancient Indian text of *The Bhagavad Gita,* Pranayam(a) is a trance-induced state where all breathing is stopped. Would you not agree, this second enhancing factor is very interesting in that it describes Samadhi, which is a possible result from undertaking or performing a long session of Kriya Kundalini Pranayam.

This is where I invite you to circle back and address the condition of and benefits of Samadhi. Specifically, the breathless state of Samadhi will naturally occur when a practitioner of Kriya Kundalini Pranayam can complete this breath with a 25-40 second breathing cycle, for 48 consecutive repetitions. The benefit of this is the body entering a state of suspended animation; a temporary state of immortality evidenced by deep brainwaves in lower theta and upper delta. We know when these brainwaves manifest themselves in a person, stress is eliminated and telomerase enzyme is produced and a state of radiant health and extended life spans are manifested.

Sometimes in Samadhi, a Kundalini awakening occurs as a massive energy infusion into the body with a corresponding experience of the fifth and sixth dimension! Kundalini is so intense the first time as to be considerably less enjoyable than in subsequent occurrences. We must not forget its primary significance is to deliver us to the doorstep of our highly desired immortality.

I am sure the question arises within you, "Can this be proven?" And the answer is "No, not at this time if you relate to shifting into higher dimensions."

However, the response would be, "Yes," if one considers the issue of altered brainwaves that are detected by brain tomography (EEG);" and another "Yes," in measuring pulse and breathing, with a pulse oximeter, which measures pulse rate and oxygen saturation in a body. Furthermore, in the people who have experienced Samadhi, there is a similarity in relating what they experienced, very similar to what occurs in near death experiences (NDE's) and descriptions from different people who have experienced in an actual temporary death.

Since I did not share the description of Kriya Kundalini Pranayam, you should be aware of a very powerful and easy-to-master breathing protocol meditation, the Tai Chi "Standing Meditation" and the practice of "Dow In". shows and explains how the Tai Chi "Standing Meditation" is performed.

In *Pathways to God: Experiencing the Energies of the Living God in Your Everyday Life* is an excellent image of how the Standing Meditation is performed. It reflects the following:

Prana/Chi/Life Force comes, or flows down, into the crown and down the spinal column to the Dantian, and then down the legs into the earth/Energy is also visualized to the area of the hands.

Complete inhaled breath into the diaphragm, golden or white in color, which is slowly exhaled, commensurate with the length of inhalation.

Arms hang loose at the side, slightly away from the body.

Ball of light collects and expands at the Dantian (energy center) with each successive inhaled breath.

Hands, fingers, and shoulders relaxed, .

Knees and elbows slightly bent

Feet: Shoulder width apart.

E.M. Energy/Prana/Chi/life force) is visualized and breathed diaphragmatically as white or gold light, that is pulled down into the Crown (TCH) and down the spinal column to the Dantian (just below the navel) where a ball of light is created, which expands with each inhaled breath). The energy/light is directed down the legs into the earth and grounds you thereto. As the light accumulates, you visualize and berate it and the exhaled breath throughout the body, including the hands. This will energize the body enough for the next parts of the Standing Meditation.

I have yet to see anyone who could not pick up this technique in a few minutes. You simply relax into a standing position, knees bent, shoulder sloped forward and hands loosely hanging by the thigh area of your body. Breathe fully into the diaphragm with your mouth closed, just above the stomach, and then exhale in an equal manner with the mouth closed.

While you execute this step, visualize a stream of white or golden light descending through the crown of your head and into the dantian (energy center) area, just above the navel. With each breath, visualize a ball of light being formed, getting bigger and more intense with each succeeding breath. Then send some of this ball of light down through your legs into the Earth. After a few minutes you will likely feel a heat and/or tingling in your hands. This is a biofeedback wherein you become more infused with Chi/Prana/life force and receive the commensurate benefits there from.

After undertaking about five to ten minutes of the "Standing Meditation," it is easy and confirming to perform the Tai Chi "Raising of the Hands," which is described herein. You can literally move your hands upward without using any muscle power, just Chi/Prana.

Note: Many of the images, and additional information supporting these activities are seen in the 2012 publication of *A Map to Healing and Your Essential Divinity Through Theta Consciousness: Physics of the Immortal "Light Body" and the Creator's Template of Perfection and Abundance for His People!*

The benefit of this additional method is to enter alpha-theta brainwaves and increase the energy of your cells and/or cellular regeneration. The same benefits are experienced in the discipline of Dow-In, which is often called a Japanese variety of Tai Chi Chuan, is performed. I am referring you once again to *Pathways to God: Experiencing the Energies of the Living God in Your Everyday Life*—and encouraging you to secure a personal study copy—the verbal instructions follow:

The raising of the hands is best accomplished by seeing oneself in a pool of water, about breast high, and the hands will naturally rise to breast high level; the elbows and knees should be slightly bent so as to not create a Chi blockage in the body.

There is yet another advanced meditation technique referred to as "The Backflow Meditation." Not for novice mediators, this technique requires a lot of concentration, visualization and breath control. Take note, the Backflow Meditation requires you to turn the pupils of your eyes upward, without tilting the head upward. This is achieved with the eyes closed, and helps to pull the meditator's consciousness back to the Medulla Oblongata, the location where the skull ends which is the soft area behind the head, below the skull. When the meditator is inhaling through the nose, the breath is brought up from the root chakra at the base of the spine and circulated to the crown concurrent with a stream of white or golden light and then directed down through the chakras on the exhaled breath through the nose. The breathing cadence is an 8-0-8-0, meaning whatever the count of your inhale, the exhale is the same amount, with no holding of the breath in between. This could be done as an 8-8-8-8, meaning each inhale for a count of 8 is followed by holding the breath for a count of 8 and then an exhale for a count of 8 and a holding of the breath for an 8 count. Either variation of this meditation creates a "spacey" feeling, with brainwaves in the theta range, and a strong cell energy infusion, which would be detected through an MTT cell assay analysis! The following images describe the meditation from the side first and from the front, secondly.

The following figures represent breathing into the diaphragm and basic meditation, and basic meditation for those people who have never meditated before or just need a refresher for such!

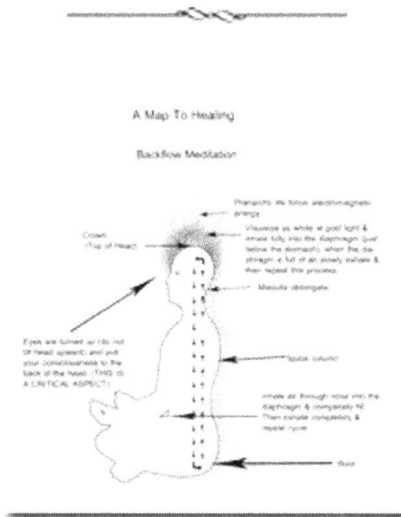

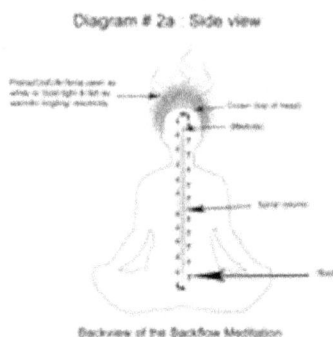

Diagram # 2a : Side view

Backview of the Backflow Meditation

Prana/chi/life force/electromagnetic energy/

Crown

Visualize as white and gold light and inhale fully into the diaphragm (just below the stomach), when the diaphragm is full of air, slowly exhale and then repeat the process.

Medulla oblongata

Eyes are turned up (do not tile head upward) and pull your consciousness to the back of the head. * This is a critical aspect.

Spiral column

Inhale air through nose into the diaphragm and completely fill. Then exhale completely and repeat cycle.

Root

It is never too late to learn to meditate. There are just too many benefits, already listed, to ignore an open avenue to higher consciousness and enhanced psychic abilities because it takes us into the alpha-theta brainwaves; brainwaves that eliminate stress and aid in the stimulation of telomerase enzyme and HGH.

Meditation in turn leads healthy telomere, continued cell replication, cellular energy infusion, human growth hormone (HGH), radiant health, extended life spans and the possibility of body immortality.

What's not to like?

DIAPHRAGMATIC BREATHING

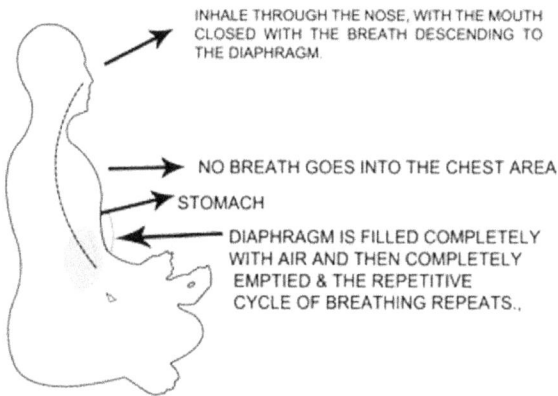

INHALE THROUGH THE NOSE, WITH THE MOUTH CLOSED WITH THE BREATH DESCENDING TO THE DIAPHRAGM.

NO BREATH GOES INTO THE CHEST AREA

STOMACH

DIAPHRAGM IS FILLED COMPLETELY WITH AIR AND THEN COMPLETELY EMPTIED & THE REPETITIVE CYCLE OF BREATHING REPEATS.,

FIG #7

What we have here is the basic meditation breathing technique of diaphragmatic breathing and the three basic meditation positions, depicted below. These are all done with an inhalation and exhalation of the breath through the nostrils of the nose, with the mouth closed. This is an 8-0-8-0 breathing regimen, which means however long is the inhaled breath, the exhaled breath should be the same duration. This is done with a mental counting and if you can extend your breath for more than a count of 8, it is even better and more beneficial to do so.

It should be mentioned that meditation can take place while a person is walking, running, dancing, involved in athletic activities, and during singing, playing and listening to music and further during the recitation of mantras, rosaries and chants. In fact many people are involved in some type of meditation without being aware they are. Activities like surfing, snowboarding and motorcycle riding especially lend themselves to a meditative state.

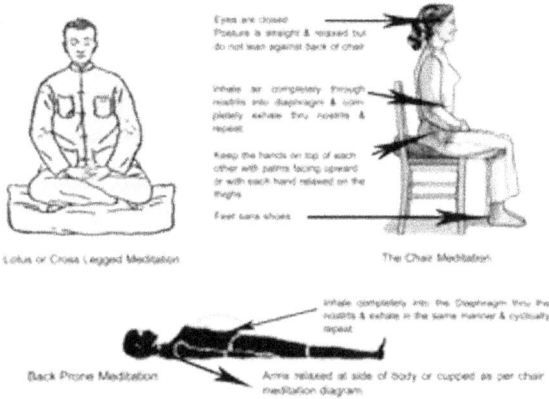

Proper Meditation Procedure For Lotus & cross legged chair, & Back Prone Lotus' & cross legged meditation position. This position is easier seated on a pillow or meditation pillow

Lotus or Cross Legged Meditation

The Chair Meditation

Back Prone Meditation

It is very easy to go to sleep in this meditation position, so it is not recommended for most meditation situations

Now it is important, actually critical, to discuss the role of exercise, Yoga Asanas (Yogic stretching), stretching, dancing, sports and extreme sports as they relate to the stimulation of telomerase enzyme. In a study by Andrew T. Ludlow, et al., titled "Relationship Between Physical Activity Level, Telomere Length and Telomerase Activity," the study disclosed it only took moderate daily exercise to increase the stimulation of telomerase enzyme. **Since all the other activities just listed are physical in** nature**, we can surmise they, too, stimulate telomerase enzyme**.

Additionally, I have personal knowledge of renowned Yogis who could perform miracles of sorts and yet when they stopped doing the Yoga Asanas (stretching), their bodies started to deteriorate at an accelerated rate and caused a hastened demise. This cannot be stressed enough: **moderate exercise of some type is crucial if we want to keep our bodies from degenerating and if we are to attain body immortality**, since not only will it stimulate the rejuvenating telomerase enzyme which vitalizes the telomere, it will **stimulate alpha and theta brainwaves** and we will feel immensely better, likewise.

Even if you consider the immortality quest to be sheer lunacy, do you consider feeling better worth pursuing?

I want to cover another concept that relates to Yoga and the previous subjects covered, known as Alchemy. Probably the foremost Alchemists of the Twentieth Century were Dr. Paul Foster Case and Carl Jung and in past times, Hermes Trismegustis/Thoth, Paracelsus, Nicolas Flamel, Robert Boyle, Roger Bacon, Sir Isaac Newton and St. Germaine... each was revered for their knowledge in this field. Now most people associate Alchemy with the process of changing lead to gold, but it seems it would be better to use tungsten, which is very close in weight to gold. Anyway, all this pales in significance to the real purpose of **Alchemy**, which is to **take the human body into a state of immortality** and so that is germane to our pursuit here.

Dr. Paul Foster Case, who wrote a definitive book on Alchemy, *The Esoteric Keys of Alchemy,* discusses using the four earth elements: water, earth, air, and fire—as well as mercury and salt—to catalyze the body into a state of immortality. And yet even he, from the Golden Dawn order of Rosicrucians, admits only just so much can be taught about the alchemicalization of the human body and the aspirant on this path must figure out the last things themselves. That is why **what is being shared here is very important, because it can align our consciousness to a state so as to make us receptive and able to perceive the exact things we need!** From the process of making Ormus, monatomic gold, with salt and oil, is one way to create this effect.

More will be mentioned about Ormus in a succeeding chapter, but it might well be the search for gold, always attached to the alchemical knowledge, which is more about creating Ormus, a gaseous form of monatomic gold, rather than to make gold from lead. Ormus has been considered a life extension agent, extending back over 400,000 years ago at a time when the Anunaki inhabited the land of Sumer in the Middle East.

Since we are always connected to the light, as per the 59th Name of God, "Hey Resh Chet" and with a certainty, to wit, as per "Resh Hey Ayin," we have the wherewithal to be receptive and perceive the knowledge we need to meet any task. Both names are from "The 72 Names of God" from *Exodus*, Chapter 14, vs. 19-21 in *The Torah;* more on this will be discussed in Chapter Three. This is being shared at this point since **there is no knowledge beyond our purview**—nothing we cannot access. Anyone who is serious about getting deeper into the study of Alchemy would be well served to get Dr. Case's monthly lessons, accessible from The Builders of the Adytum, who disseminate the Ageless Wisdom of Sacred Tarot and Holy Qabalah. These lessons in Tarot, Numerology and *The 72 Names of God* (from Exodus) will provide the esoteric/spiritual components of Alchemy, the finest points of which can only be learned through personal experience and intuitional (psychic) guidance/Divine guidance.

Now, let's take a break and shift our thoughts to the cymatic, vibrational, sound factors that stimulate telomerase enzyme, in Chapter Three, and digest all the information we tackled in this chapter, whew! Let's break things up with another poem in the next chapter!

| CHAPTER THREE

LET ME ASK YE, DO YOU WANT TO BE FREE AND LIVE LIKE A TREE? THEN MANTRAS MIGHT BE FOR THEE!

———⟨∞⟩———

Many times have I been asked if I would worship a tree,
My response has been… they are unfettered and free.
Even when damaged and wounded they be,
Never will they complain or wish to flee,
From the condition in which they may reside.
So engrossed in perfection from which they do not hide,
In a state of bliss and divinity they ever abide.
Without them, who would be our constant guide?
They guide us to a God in whom we can confide.
Dr. Robert Newton, 10-28-15

———⟨∞⟩———

FEW PEOPLE IN the scheme of creation, place trees, plants, and animals, are higher on the scale of divinity than human beings! This perception seems to exist because some descriptions of the creation of Earth state humans were given dominion over the Earth. To assume the word dominion means now what it did at the ascribed date of the Creation of *The Torah* and *The Old Testament* is an incorrect assumption and presumptuous, to wit. Five thousand years ago, at the time these particular books are believed to have been created, **the word "dominion" meant something more akin to "stewardship" as opposed to the control** and indiscriminate use of and superiority it means in the 21st Century. Well explained in a Jain sutra, this means that *all beings exist to be mutually beneficial to each other*.

This gives those of us who feel all the creations of Nature are something more magnificent, or at the very least equal to humans, some solid ground upon which to stand. It is **irrevocably true that trees can live without humans but most certainly, humans cannot live without the many benefits of trees share with us, asking nothing in return,** as well. So the least we can do to these presences, which are clearly superior to us, is to treat them with respect... and that means not butchering them on the rationale we are doing them a favor, or because the leaves that fall from the tree are a nuisance or huge inconvenience! Consider just what trees do for humans: they sequester carbon dioxide and convert it to oxygen, fix or infuse carbon into the soil making it more fertile, create shade, lower ambient temperatures, break or lower the force of winds, and provide us with fruit and lumber. Did I miss anything?

Even more impressive than this, a tree does not need to eat food—but rather produces energy outside the parameter of ingesting food—through photosynthesis. This process occurs when sunlight interacts with water inside a tree and creates chlorophyll, which is used as food/energy. Later in Chapters Six and Ten, we will discover if humans are capable of the same thing.

Trees live free, meaning unrestrained by stress, injury, a fear of death and focus on making a "joyful noise unto the Lord," via a type of singing/toning, which has actually been recorded, as in the singing plants at Damanhur.

These might be perceived as mantras, because there is a repeating of the sounds just as are in mantras/rosaries. This amazing synchronicity would give a type of validation as to the value of human mantras. These synchronicities manifest themselves as above and below—and below and above—via the atomic forms of creation being manifested on the human Earth level and up to the galactic level and reversed from top to bottom, likewise; and it also manifests sideways, too, as we process the similarities in plants, animals and humans as we are finding in the geometries of fractal forms.

As amazing and beneficial as are our trees, humans, in contradistinction, manage to pollute almost everything on planet Earth and are buffeted about by the smallest and most irrelevant things… really we are in need of singing to balance our emotions. Yet the trees just know inherently to do so, whereas humans have to have a song and dance dialogue, as it were, to reach the same realization and still will doubt the validity and usefulness of these sounds.

The real reason for this digression into a discussion of trees is to reiterate trees and plants have been measured as emanating sounds, singing, toning, akin to music. These sounds are quite ethereal and there is a strong possibility the trees are benefited physically and emotionally, as are humans likewise. **These sounds might also have something to do with the long life spans exhibited by trees**; in fact trees exhibit a guiding intuition that few humans ever experience except when they are in a state of Samadhi, as was previously mentioned. It should be added, this breathless state of Samadhi can lead not only to immortality but also to a state of euphoria and bliss that is very addictive and satisfying, like nothing else humans ever experience, except during a sexual orgasm.

Continuing to move forward with this discussion... the data on how certain sounds and the cymatic or vibrational effects there from, influence humans, is well documented. To be precise, we know the vowel sounds in Sanskrit and Hebrew—even though Hebrew does not technically have vowels yet vowel sounds are effectively produced when speaking Hebrew—create alpha and theta brain waves, de-stress the human body and subsequently lead to the stimulation of telomerase enzyme, keeping our telomere functioning at a high level, and create HGH to provide improved health and extended life spans. These sounds will also infuse our body cells with more energy or cell vitality, which an MMR scan will reveal.

Addressing the first of three Sanskrit Mantras that will be covered, "Aum," is known as the "primal sound of creation."

It has eight distinct geometric forms created by its sound. The pictures below illustrate such. These eight geometric forms are created by the Sanskrit mantra, "Aum." They are represented in the following Fig 7.

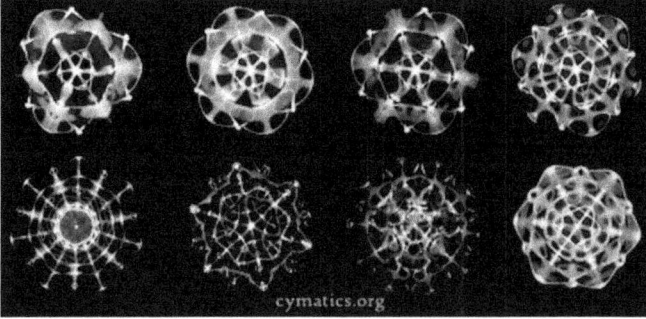

FIG# 8

The next Sanskrit mantra we will look at is the "Gayatri Mantra," which has come to be known as the "Mother of all mantras." In India, almost everyone knows this mantra; some children learning it as young as three or four years old. As important as this mantra is known to be, almost no one in India has seen the geometric intricacy from this mantra, which just happens to be "The Shree Yantra".

The mantra that follows, is phonetically translated:

Aum Bhur Bhuvah Suvaha,
Tat Savithur Varenyam,
Bhargo Devsaya Dhimahee,
Dhiyo Yonah Prochodiat.

FIG #9

The Shree Yantra is actually produced by having a speaker under a table of sand, playing "The Gayatri Mantra."

The other Sanskrit mantra I cover is known as "The Maha Mrityunjaya." Measuring the energy of this mantra with dowsing rods on someone who has performed it reveals a vastly increased auric or energy field. This mantra is shared in *A Map to Healing and Your Essential Divinity Through Theta Consciousness*. The same thing occurs with the dowsing rods when "The Gayatri Mantra" and "Aum Mantras" are recited. Now as exciting and propitious this is, we have even more cymatic effects to examine, which just happens to be another language, with cymatic or vibrational properties, known as Hebrew. In the Hebrew language, we find the "The 72 Names of God,' from "Exodus" in *The Torah*. There is a powerful healing protocol using these "72 Names of God" discussed in my work, *A Map to Healing and Your Essential Divinity Through Theta Consciousness*. Fig. 10 is a chart of these cymatically powerful names of God.

FIG #10

Let's now look at the **cymatic/vibrational effects of both Hebrew and Sanskrit on the atomic level of creation**. It is through the following photos we gain more insight into the power of these languages. The value of these is in the effect on the human body and mind, with a higher tuning of the human body through atoms that are forced to move faster and the geometric lattices they form; and with alpha-theta brainwaves being created, an overall body relaxation leading to the elimination of stress and a resulting telomerase enzyme generation. What more could we ask for? How about human growth hormone (HGH)? Yes, in fact, HGH is produced! Does it become evident we effectively get something of great value without having to pay anything to get such?

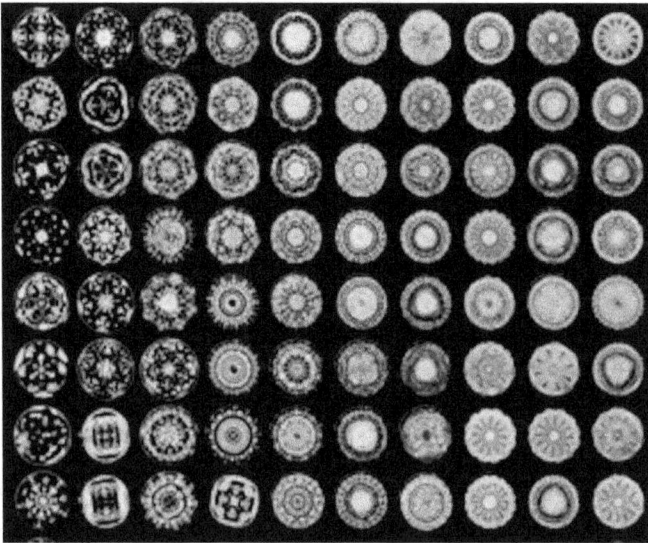

FIG #11

In the left three columns of Fig. 11 we have the atomic geometries of Sanskrit and in the remaining seven columns, we have the atomic geometries of Hebrew. Notice the great similarity in the geometric forms being created by the sounds of each language. Such a synchronicity/coincidence provides cross validation of the cymatic/vibrational power of each language... both Sanskrit and Hebrew.

Let us also examine the cymatic power related to all of this, namely the six notes of the Solfeggio frequencies, a non diatonic scale in which "The Gregorian Chants" were written. Each frequency has strong effects on the human body and mind but the 528-Hertz frequency has been ascertained as the most powerful note within this Solfeggio scale. Most notable is the **similarity between the atomic geometric forms created by the Solfeggio frequencies and the atomic geometries of Sanskrit and Hebrew.**

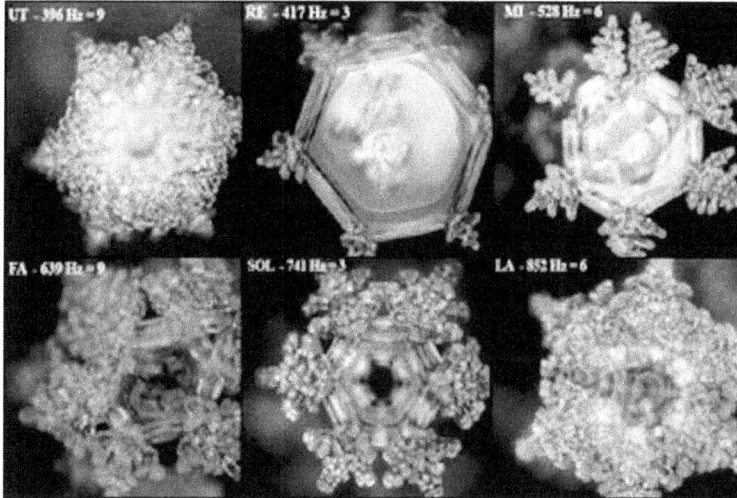

FIG #12

Robert J. Newton

The atomic geometries revealed in the cymatics of vibrations in the Solfeggio Frequencies look hauntingly similar to Dr. Emoto's water crystal pictures where the intent and energy of Love was infused into the water, and in fact they were.

There is also a synchronicity, a resonance if you will... an overlay between this 528-Hertz frequency or note and the Schuman Earth Resonance frequency of 7.83 Hertz. There is not an exactly resonance at 7.83 Hertz but there is in the oscillation of the Shuman resonance field as it oscillates above and below its 7.83 Hertz base frequency. Why this is important, for our purposes, is the more similarities we can establish between various frequencies, the more evidence we have of the validity of the concept, the more power with which we can ascribe to it, and the more confidence we can have that we have found useful tools in the quest for vastly improved health and longer life spans—immortality, itself!

For further support related to this, Nick Anthony Fiorenza writes in *432 Hertz and the Schuman Resonance that* 8 Hertz = the note C4 = 430.54 Hertz and is very close mathematical connection between 7.83 Hertz, the Shuman Resonance and the Solfeggio frequency of 528 Hertz and the diatonic 432 Hz. frequency. If your curiosity mounts, you might question, "Is there power and force in specific frequencies?" In fact, this very issue has been revealed herein and as an aside, American inventor, John Keely, used the notes of the diatonic scale to power perpetual motion machines. Just know **there is a power in the frequencies covered... sufficient to stimulate telomerase enzyme and**

repair the telomeres in the chromosomes of the DNA and to manufacture HGH.

Distilled, as per the cymatic factors, 7.83 Hz. = 528 Hz. – 430-432 Hz. and will there will be a roughly equivalent cymatic power between them. The conclusion to which this should lead us to is: if we perform the designated Sanskrit mantras daily, at 108 continuous recitations and repeating the *72 Names of God,* in conjunction with the vibrational frequencies just mentioned, our brains/minds will be filled with alpha and theta brainwaves, and a resultant production of telomerase enzyme and HGH.

It must be mentioned that **the atomic geometries and their cymatic/vibrational effects, which emanate from Sanskrit and Hebrew have a soothing effect on our emotions and reduce an eliminate stress** in our lives. Just as important, they transport our bodies into more of a state of light and less to a state of dense matter. Additionally, there is a shift in brain-mind consciousness because of the alpha and theta brainwaves as a result of the cymatic effect of Hebrew and Sanskrit, providing no less least three benefits from the recitations. Pause for a moment and consider, "Is this process something that will move us forward to immortalizing our bodies?" The conclusion? Could we say, certainly it will be more than useful?

With this topic having been satisfactorily covered, let us shift our focus to the power of numbers as we address the inter-relationships between numbers, and why they are useful for the purpose of stimulating telomerase enzyme.

| Chapter Four

Dare we ask for more?
Ask and ye shall receive, and in numbers
shall we find colour!

On the road to physical immortality,

It might not be so easy for the way to see,

Coursing along a path to be truly free,

Befriended by old and twisted Cedar tree,

I found an insight that set me free!

As I contemplated the meaning of words,

I realized this was beyond the knowledge of herds,

I would have to look at numbers and their constant meaning,

Having things revealed to me beyond just a mere gleaning,

As I let go of my confusion there would be a weaning.

In my understanding would be clarity and cleaning.

Dr. Robert Newton, 10-30-15

Robert J. Newton

THE MAIN PROBLEM with most languages, other than Sanskrit, is they are rife with ambiguity from the high level abstractions that are inherent therein, yet bandied about in a cavalier fashion with the assumption these words have a universally accepted meaning when in fact such a notion is pure folly. English, the language used here, is within the group of ambiguous, highly abstracted, languages and the field of General Semantics, pioneered by S.I Hayakawa, is embodied by the phrase uttered by Hayakawa, *"The word is not the thing."* If we consider the language common to us, it becomes self evident that the "word" truly is only a symbol for "a thing."

I have been blessed to meet Lee Ross, Chris Dillard—founder and curator, respectively—and their group, Temple of Objective Life Study (T.O.O.L.S). The duo created what I consider to be an amazingly insightful treatise, which can be viewed at www.t-o-o-l-s.net. They used the concept of numbers and mathematics, known as **Gematria, to counteract the "ambiguity factors" and give us powerful insights into words not otherwise available.** So let's be adventurous and look at some specific words.

First we will consider the word immortal. So we know, more than less, "immortal" means living forever and thus this would seem to be an adequate description, thereof. Yet when we look at synonym words, numerically, we start to see beyond things obtuse, not readily apparent from the word and words themselves, for example:

The Immortality Prophecy

1. The number 101 equals the sum of all numerals of "immortal" using the letter "A" as the number one and ascending one letter and one number at a time to the letter "Z" at 26.

2. 101 also represents the numeral exchange for the word love in Greek, the Hebrew word, Mikal, which is interchangeable with the Arch Angel Michael, and the phrase "son of God."

3. Additionally, 101 also denotes other common phrases such as universal energies, personal development, and spiritual awakening.

I would have you, then, consider how this would indicate to us if we want to be "immortal" we would concentrate on very powerful words of the Greek word "love," "the Arch Angel Michael," and the "son of God," etc. Additionally, we would gravitate to the qualities and personages that could help us achieve a state of immortality. Further, the word love equates numerally to light—it is that exact love and light that takes us in the direction of being immortal… at the very least, that is what the numbers are telling us!

How could we ever decipher these possibilities without gaining and using the numerical insights of Gematria? We would be clueless otherwise about these relevant connections! It should be mentioned that in the writings of J.G. R. Forlong, found in Rivers of Life, the author describes the Ark of Phile, an object located in the past in Egypt, and things associated with the number "101." It is presumed if the Ark were to be found, it would hold keys to the body immortal as well.

Looking to deconstruct the number "101", we find the number "1" equates to the following:

God force	*initiative*	*attainment*
new beginnings	*assertiveness*	*achieving success*
creativity	*intuition*	*personal fulfillment*
creation	*inspiration*	
motivation	*happiness*	
progress	*positivity*	

Thus cultivating and utilizing these attributes might well move us closer to achieving a state of the body immortal. Literally, we manifest in our lives what we focus on and surround ourselves with, as per my conversations with readers in *A Map to Healing and Your Essential Divinity Through Theta Consciousness*. In short, **the programming in our brain, mind, or personal computer-brain is what we can expect to be manifested in our lives.**

Think about this... what might transfer should we consider changing our names equaling the numeral total of 101? It is conceivable the change would bring the 101 vibrations into an active presence in our lives. This is not mentioned in a flippant manner but rather something to be seriously considered.

The Immortality Prophecy

Now let's see what "0" equals in words, including:

universal energies

eternity

infinity

oneness

wholeness

beginning point

continuation of cycles and flow

developing spiritual aspects

listening to intuition and higher self to find answers

Again, cultivating these qualities and demonstrating them in our lives will serve to put us in alignment with immortalizing our bodies.

Continuing this process: start by adding the numbers, and you find 1 + 0 + 1 equals 2. This just happens to be an "angel number," and we will be examining angels in the next chapter. We would also find this in the number "110" as well as "101." It should be apparent there are just too many guideposts, guidelines, or insights—whatever you feel inclined to call them—for us to ignore the numeral insights that Gematria give us—providing certain directions and synonyms that can guide us to immortality. Being as frank as possible, I ask you to recognize the enormous negative morphogenic field of energy established on Earth, which makes our immortality quest more difficult than it would—if there were more people who believed immortality was in fact within the realm of the achievable—as was known in India, Atlantis, Sumeria, Egypt and Lemuria before the existing timelines of archaeology.

Utilizing numeral insights gives us a more "level playing field" to make immortality a more realistic venture. Literally, through **using the synonyms related to immortality we are establishing morphic fields of supporting energy to make our quest easier and surer to achieve!** With this let us then consider additional factors in the next chapter... where we question whether angels aid us in our quest for immortality.

There is another aspect to numbers, apart from their association with words, and that is the interrelationship between them. Edward Leedskalninm, the creator of "Coral Castle," using megalithic blocks of coral, proposed one such association. No one ever discovered how Leedskalninm moved these large multi-ton pieces of coral into place. He shared, however, his secrets were in 7129 Hertz (Hz) + 610 Hz. + 5195 Hz. That equals 12934 Hz. Using the power of numbers, they reduce to 19 and then 10, and finally break down to 1 and 0. Remember the discussion of these numbers, earlier in this chapter, and remember they are powerful, indeed... to the gate of immortality, 101! The discussion must continue, by asking other questions: Is the power of levitating objects, such as what Leedskalninm did with large coral blocks, in the group of numbers? Is the key to immortalizing a human body, likewise, contained therein? We can numerically view the questions another way and take the total of the sequences, 19 +7 +20, which equal 46; its inverse is 64. The number 46 just happens to be the atomic number of Palladium, a highly active metal that is used in the process of "cold fusion." There are 46 chromosomes and 46 is considered a "pure number." So, can we use the highly active properties of Palladium and our chromosomes to guide us into a state of immortality? It certainly should be considered an active lead!

This concept can also be confirmed by the word for "truth" in Hebrew, which equals the inverse of 46, 64. Cross validating evidence has more force and effect than any human opinion or theory, something we can reliably depend upon.

As you may know, genius inventor, Nikola Tesla, tells us the secret to everything lies in the numbers 3, 6, and 9, which are integers of 3. The numbers 1, 2, 3, 4, 5, 6, 7, and 8 are included in this "sacred interval." In the study of numbers, we find 3, 6, and 9 equal 18—and with an inverse of 81, they all reduce back to 9. Does invoking these numbers aid in the process of immortality? Was Tesla's harnessing of the electromagnetic field of energy AKA Prana and Chi and God life force related to 3,6, and 9? Does this relate to a human harnessing this omnipresent energy into a body immortal?

Further, there are some sacred numbers in the amino acids of A, C, T, and G of our DNA; they equal 31 and the inverse of this is 13. Now, it just so happens that $13 \times 2 = 26$ and 26 just happens to equal the representation of God. This would further indicate our DNA may well be a double dose of God, as manifested in the double helix of the DNA.

Now… let us ascend to the realm of angels.

| Chapter Five

Angel Jive and new Angels arrive, so in angels our bodies may abide.

In the midst of angels we always are,
Their presence is for our use and never far.
When we are in dire need of real help,
They are there for us and we need not yelp!
Dr. Robert Newton, 10-31-15

THE NEXT UNCOVERING will be directed to the numerical aspects of angels, which are rife with possibilities relative to our immortality search. There are numerous angels on the Kabbalistic *Tree of Life*. At least two of these listed angels, positioned at the top of the hierarchy of this *Tree of Life,* are Archangel Michael/Mickel and Metatron/Enoch. Enoch lived a faultless life in his incarnations on Earth and was invited to the highest realms of Heaven, by the supreme God, to sit next to his Creator, as Metatron.

It is not well known; however... Enoch lived different lives as Enoch in Palestine; as Thoth in Sumer and Egypt; Tehuti in Atlantis; Hermes Trismegustis in Greece; and Quetzocoatl in Central America and possibly even Peru and other parts of South America, and as Merlin in England. What is well documented is his accomplishments at these places are legendary.

I share the following with you to reveal the character and power of Enoch and his other permutations/personages. Every country where Enoch was present was vastly benefited there from. So we can affirmatively state Metatron, Enoch, and/or other incarnations of this personage was at the highest level of spiritual attainment, knowledge and abilities. Additionally, he created the hieroglyphic symbols and language in Egypt. He helped establish the early government in Egypt and was instrumental in instruction the Egyptian priests with esoteric knowledge, and wrote *The Egyptian Book of the Dead* as well as *The Emerald Tablet* and *The Corpus Hermeticum* in Greece. He was central figure in the esoteric knowledge of the Olmecs, of the first major civilization in Mexico, and the Toltecs, Aztecs and Mayas of Central American—and most likely in South America as well. The multi-personality Enoch, besides having been exalted as Metatron, is considered a marker—a guide—to an immortalized body since even before becoming Metatron, Enoch had already transcended the state of death and was living in a Merkaba/Merkabah/body of light.

It has been related in some texts, Archangel Michael was responsible for aiding Enoch in turning his body in a ball of light, a Merkabah of sorts. We know Michael has always

76

been associated with "The Solar Cross" and the Sun and he exists in a ball of light also known as a Merkabah. He is also known as "The Universal Protector," or someone who is always ready to protect and support those who invoke his presence. Throughout history, such invocation would be done by simply invoking Michael's name vocally or by visualizing him.

How does this relate to immortalizing a human body into a body of light or a Merkabah? Simply, those who have pulled this off are the very ones who can aid us and light our path, as it were, to our goal! A morphogenic field/a morphic field (a pattern/template of energy existing and accessible) is created for this specific task and for each succeeding aspirant it makes the task easier to complete, as per Ken Keyes book, *The Hundredth Monkey* and Dr. Rupert Sheldrake's *A New Science of Life*. In a nutshell, what Sheldrake promotes is everything that occurs is recorded in the field of atoms, possibly even stored in a "Cosmic Computer" in a central part of the Universe, and which is further noted in Dr. J.J. Hurtak's *The Keys of Enoch*.

Once this information and/or pattern, template, or form is established, it is thus easier for each succeeding person to accomplish.

The first person to accomplish something always works harder the their successors. So take heart in the knowledge that a trail or trails have already been blazed, which we can follow with less effort than the pioneer who first demarked the path/paths.

The 59th Name of God from *The 72 Names of God* from "Exodus 14, vs. 19-21" is "Hey Resh Chet" means connected to the light. There would be a natural connection between this name and the solar presence of Archangel Michael. Additionally, the angel corresponding with this name of God is "Harahel" who is also known as the patron of intellectual richness—gives us access to knowledge.

In consonance with these angel, light, and/or sun connections, we have *The Gayatri Mantra,* in Sanskrit, which is exaltation to Savitur/Sun/God/Shiva. The real power from reciting this mantra comes from reciting it continuously 108 times, as per Hindu and Yogic traditions. This mantra was already shared in Chapter Three, but if you need a refresher... **the Sanskrit language has cymatic or vibrational power that creates the atomic geometries, which give us access to the higher dimensions beyond a third dimension Earth operating system.** The vital point made here is this being the exact type of impetus that immortalizing a body entails since it is in the higher dimensions where this occurs... dimensions more infused with a higher energy field and the corresponding light emanated from a higher concentration of photons.

There is another Sanskrit mantra, T*he Maha Mrityunjaya Mantra,* which is also an exaltation of the Sun. As with *The Gayatri Mantra, its* highest benefit is unlocked by reciting it continuously for 108 repetitions. There are the same cymatic benefits leading to the operating systems accessed in the higher dimensions, wherein a light body/Merkabah/immortal body can exist and flourish and belongs, to wit! This mantra is as follows in phonetic English:

Aum triumbakum yajamahee,

Segundum puushte varenaam,

Uvardacam eva bandenat,

Mritshore muksheya mamretat

Beyond using the Sanskrit mantras and the Name of God discussed, "Hey Resh Chet," the question lies in how we would invoke more sun and more light into our lives to give us the extra push necessary to increase sun and light factors in our bodies. **If you want the divine power of the Sun, you must immerse yourself therein.** While the Sun has been associated with skin cancer, in fact a human body does not operate very well without a sufficient quotient of its benefits, including Vitamin D. Depending on what part of the day you draw in the sun, it could involve as little as fifteen minutes to half an hour, just after sunrise or just before sunset, sunbathing with minimal or no clothing. This could also be done in the prime time of the day—if you are not fearful of getting skin cancer. Use muscle kinesiology to determine your course of action.

Sun gazing is another Sun energy accumulating factor. The Sun should only be gazed into during the sunrise/sunset parameters due to possible negative effects to the eyes. Doing this twice per day at the sunrise/sunset would offer more benefit than done once per day. **For both sunbathing and sun gazing, the amount of time devoted to these activities**

should be ascertained by muscle kinesiology, irrespective of what is otherwise advised!

Chapter Two was a discussion of various meditations with Prana/Chi augmentation properties for the human body. The Tai Chi "Standing Meditation" was one of those Prana energy amplifiers, as well as Qui Gong and Kriya Kundalini Pranayam(a). I draw your attention back to these meditations because, as much as the sunbathing and sun gazing will allow more Sun/Prana/Chi to be stored in the body, the benefit from the Tai Chi "Standing Meditation" Qui Gong and Kriya Kundalini Pranayam will provide more value in enhancing the light/Prana/Chi quotient in your body. The activity is supported by the information detailed on page 369 of the Paramahansa Yogananda translation of *The Bhagavad Gita*. This work talks about the **Yagna (fire) and Agna (light and Aum (the primordial sound of creation and amen) comprising the Intelligent Cosmic Vibration Yagna,** which was discussed in the earlier chapter. When a person performs a Kriya Kundalini Pranayam breathing meditation or Kundalini Yoga breathing, the Prana, comprised of fire and light, is being breathed into the body and distributed there about and even stored therein.

It may appear I strayed away from the angel connection and the benefits thereof in discussing other topics; however, this is not the case because I want to impress upon you that **if you want the immortality of an angel, comprised only of atoms, manifesting as fire and light, you must practice those things that allow you to access the level of angels.** Another salient angel connection, something of great note, is the angel Achaiah, known as one of the Seraphim, and the angel of patience, who is related to the Seventh Name of God, "Aleph Kaf Aleph," which represents the restoration of things to their perfect state. Since a body of light, a Merkabah, in the fourth and fifth-dimensions is more perfect in operation and movement than a body of dense light, as we have in the third-dimension, there is a great benefit in being able to establish one's body and consciousness, at least, in the fourth dimension, if not higher. **The more Agna (light) and Yagna (fire) stored in a body, the more perfect it becomes.**

To invoke the name of Achaiah would allow us to access a path to a perfect, immortal body. This would come from insights and instructions we would receive in a meditative state with the corresponding brainwaves of alpha and theta that can be produced in deep meditation.

There is another connection with an exalted figure from *The Old Testament/Torah* in the form of Elijah, not considered an angel—yet maybe so—who went to heaven in a "chariot" light, a Merkabah. So again, in a morphic sense, and fortuitous for us, our task has been made easier to immortalize our so-called physical bodies. Elijah might well have been a previous incarnation of Jesus. When the crowds asked Jesus who he was, he replied, "Some say I am Elisha and others say I am Elijah," leaving us to ponder whether Jesus pulled off His body light twice. According to his own words, quite possibly this is in fact true.

This conversation naturally leads us to the next chapter about what really nourishes a human body. Is it food or is there some outside nutrifying factor, beyond the metabolism of food?

| Chapter Six

If we stop eating food, will we really be putting out body in a "fix" so we need to keep our chop sticks?

We have all been taught food is a must,

If we do not eat it we will return to dust,

Yet when we look into what food itself really is,

It is essentially the energy there from that gives us the fizz.

We know that food supplies us with power,

But what about Prana, is it too an "energy shower?"

The breathairian practitioner learns not to cower,

If there be no food they be not disempowered

Dr. Robert Newton, 11-02-15

PART OF ENTERING a state of immortalizing the body is that it no longer needs food to sustain the energy/light body. In fact, we all are, already, a body of energy and light; however, due to the programs in our minds we believe we are dense matter and will perish without food. In fact, there are many people who are fanatic about eating food to keep their bodies fueled and maintaining their blood sugar/glucose levels. We look to the consideration of Adeno diphosphate (ADP), an important organic compound in metabolism, which is fundamental to the flow of energy in living cells, and creates Adeno triphosphate (ATP), which in turn creates energy from the food we consume. **Perhaps the more important question is whether we can metabolize energy from the air, water, light and fire we are surrounded by and literally comprised there from.**

Looking carefully at Fig 13, it begs the question, "Have you ever noticed in the pictures of Jesus, St. Germaine, Krishna, Rama, Babaji Nagaraj and Buddha, there is usually this band of light above the head of these personages and often around the body too?" This is commonly known as an aura, which is the real energy essence of a body.

Photo Attribution:
Yogini Ashram

Then you might know that when a body dies and the soul makes a transition to another dimension, **there is not an aura displayed around that body unless said body is in a state of "super suspension"** such as with the body of Mary Baker

Eddy, author of *Science and Health with Key to the Scriptures* and Paramahansa Yogananda, founder of "The Self Realization Fellowship." Their bodies did not deteriorate even nine months after they passed on, which would indicate an aura there about, which is just how the body of Paramahansa Yogananda was described by those who viewed it... basically surrounded by light, an aura.

Kriya Kundalini Yoga Satguru Babaji Nagaraj, established in Soruba Samadhi since 205 A.D., means he entered a breathless state of bliss, needing neither food nor breath to remain in a state of bodily immortality.

What I propose here is that no body can be sustained without this auric field surrounding it.

This represents auric energy, or etheric energy, which is electromagnetic energy that can be measured with an electrometer, or a very sensitive voltmeter and dowsing rods.

The electromagnetic energy is comprised of atoms, with their positive (+) and negative (-) electrical charges and this said electrical energy, known also as Prana, Chi, Orgone, Ka, Ba, or Eloptic energy. Energy is what the human body is comprised of and powered by much more so than the food we eat that we believe nutrifies us.

What if it was possible to just live of Prana or Chi, irrespective of food intake? In fact it is and is being done as you read this. What has been previously covered in this book, is the key to such, including Kriya Kundalini Pranayam, the

Robert J. Newton

Tai Chi "Standing Meditation," Qui Gong, Sanskrit mantras, *The 72 Names of God,* sunbathing and sun gazing are precise and certain ways to infuse the body with Prana/Chi.

I first discussed this in my book, *A Map to Healing and Your Essential Divinity Through Theta Consciousness, in Chapter Eleven.*

In his documentary, *In the Beginning There was Light,* Peter Arthur Straubinger, filmed two Breatharians in a hospital setting with twenty four hour closed circuit TV monitoring, with each participant being hooked up to medical monitors, it was clearly revealed it was possible to live vibrantly, not just languish, in a condition of no food or water intake for a period of two weeks. One participant was certified to have not eaten in seventy years and the other not eating for seven years. Vital sign measurements were taken both before and after the two-week period and to the astonishment of the medical personnel, who supervised this study in a hospital; there was no degeneration in either subject. Before this test, the medical personnel were derisively proclaiming how these two men would be very adversely affected by their ordeal. Afterward, they were dumbfounded when the opposite occurred. Not only was no degeneration experienced by these men's bodies, they were in a state of complete health.

Is it being suggested that right away the readers of this book immediately become Breatharians? Emphatically no, absolutely not, and not because it cannot be done but rather **we must first change the programming in our**

brain/mind/personal-computer so that we are not working against ourselves, with some manner of subconscious interference, or self-sabotage! Remember, we have been programmed our entire lives we need to eat to survive on planet Earth. Earlier in this treatise, we discussed mind reprogramming. First, you would need to eliminate the beliefs from your mind you need food and water to sustain yourself. This is crucial and yet this is a pervasive belief on planet Earth! It affects us unless we have expunged the idea and replaced our belief with something that allows us to reach our goal, specifically... that we can thrive without food! So I refer you once again to *A Map to Healing and Your Essential Divinity Through Theta Consciousness* for directions re mind reprogramming, in Chapter Four, therein.

The next part of our journey is to look into the medical contraindications to Breathairianism; **I also caution you that this process should never be undertaken without the advice of a qualified doctor!** Unfortunately, the problem remains that is there probably are very few, if any doctors, who would ever advise venturing down the path of Breathairianism, so you might need to make this decision yourself. Remember it is **essential to reprogram your own mind** or engage the services of a highly experienced hypnotherapist, theta healer, theta consciousness reprogramming practitioner, etc. Ultimately, this is a life changing decision that is yours, and you must take responsibility for such. I wish our societies did not put us in legal peril for all of our statements, but *se la vie!* Such are the perils of the Uniform Commercial Code and the onerous Admiralty Law that comes therewith.

The following is a valuable resource, which allows us to take the leap to move into breatharianism and reprogram our minds to accept such. In *The American Journal of Clinical Nutrition,* Dr. Paul Webb and his associates published a groundbreaking article regarding their studies in Calorimetry (the study and measuring of caloric energy), which indicated **23% of the energy powering a human body came from non-food or non-caloric sources!** Dr. Webb also investigated 52 other studies related to this subject and found the same results occurred. Webb's breakthrough contradicted the findings of Antoine Lavoisier, Rene Descartes, Atwater and Benedict— which the body works like an inorganic machine where the amount of calories a body would need could be predicted— when in fact there was never any standard formula for their premise that has been discovered, yet alone proposed.

We next look to Durnin, et al., and Dr. William Riggins, in *The Myth of the Calorie,* whose findings confirmed those of Dr. Webb, revealing the body was at least partly maintained by energy from outside of the body, beyond that produced by the energy for food.

———————

We inquire, "Could that outside of the body energy source be Prana/Chi/ God life force? Is this energy electromagnetic energy? Does this energy come from our Soul?"

Let's investigate further! Can Prana or Chi solely power the body? In fact, let's take it so far as to ask, **"Is it possible all the energy that powers a body could come from non-caloric sources?"** Let us use an analogy from other organic sources such as trees and plants. Trees and plants regularly take sunlight and turn it into chlorophyll via the process of photosynthesis, through sunlight interacting with water in the tree leaves in conjunction with the element, iron. The chlorophyll is the food and yet the tree or plant does not have to eat it to become nourished; rather **there is a chemical reaction between light and water and iron to create nourishing chlorophyll**, which is moved vascularly through the tissues of the tree.

What factor or force then would prevent a human body taking energy from the Sun or the Agna and Yagna, the light and the fire—or these same things generated during Kriya Kundalini Pranayam—and converting that into a human chlorophyll of sorts and powering the body there from?

Before summarily dismissing this notion, keep in mind this process of nutrification has already been formulated as an operating system by the Creator for trees and plants and just because a human has a mouth which can masticate food, that does not preempt a photosynthesis of sorts for humans! Lo and behold! In number of articles by Herrera, et al., posted by Dr. Gerald Pollack, in fact **there is scientific proof of a process similar to plant photosynthesis that occurs within the bodies of humans.**

This happens in two ways, as related by Dr. Gerald Pollack. The first being: how the melanin (not melatonin) in a human body reacts with sunlight, to produce an electrical reaction in the body that stimulates energy therein. The other way is when sunlight interacts with the water inside our bodies, of which there are ample amounts, totaling about 65%; the main element in the human body. This **interaction of sunlight and even Prana with water and magnesium and creates what is called, EZ Water,** also recognized as H_3O_2 water; this in turn creates an alkaline condition in the body, which creates energy like an alkaline battery and draws on its natural plus and negative charges to circulating energy/electricity. This seems to be the source that allows ATP to be created and then fuel our bodies. This process is called oxidative phosphorylation.

Voilà! We learn **water is not just water.** Which brings up another reality: the bulk water delivered in our municipal water systems is not only full of toxins—it is energetically dead. There is another problem with these bulk waters and that is an overabundance of Deuterium, a heavy hydrogen element that lowers the energy potential inside a body. Yet **water from streams, glaciers and deep water wells is infused with H3O2** and a lot of energy and low in Deuterium, as well, according to Dr. Pollack. He has researched and studied this special water, and reveals H_3O_2 is the type of water found within our cells, when they are healthy and it flows much easier than H_2O. Granted, Dr. Pollack sells the EZ-water producing units through his company, Structured Water; however. Dr. Pollack does not claim you can live only on this water without food—only that this water leads to more energy and better health.

I do ask, however, "Can we live on EZ-water alone? If our cells are functioning perfectly, why couldn't we do this, irrespective of no glucose/glycogen being produced? "**Is there glucose or some nutrifying sugar in this water... or a molecule H3O2, infused with more hydrogen and oxygen atoms able to replace glucose and glycogen?**" It would appear, in fact, the H_3O_2 serves this replacement purpose.

You will find this is where things get really interesting learning of Dr. Albert Szent-Gyorgyi's discovery hydrogen increases energy in the human body through catalyzing ATP (Adeno triphosphate) and releasing fuel for the body. Even more importantly, or at least as significantly, Australian decathlon champion, John O'Neill found a way to fuel his athletic activities through using hydrogen in the place of glycogen/glucose. O'Neill is **able to prevent the buildup of lactic acid in his muscles and vastly extend the length of his athletic performance using hydrogen**, going into the Hydrogen efficiency zone (HEZ) Is he using EZ-water (H_3O_2)? I have not ascertained this yet; however there are hydrogen supplements marketed by *Dancing with Water* added to the body through supplements and liquid hydrogen. Remember, liquid hydrogen was used to power many missiles in the NASA flights and very combustive it was, for sure, which means there is a high energy potential in the element, hydrogen.

Let's address what has an excess of hydrogen in molecular form. Could it be H_3O_2? Indeed it is, and the extra atom of oxygen enables the combustion of hydrogen. Is this just a coincidence? I would stand affirmed that coincidences really are not a part of an intelligently designed Universe and we have already documented that intelligence and design are manifested in the nine geometric forms of creation and the various type of sounds waves on the atomic level. Further, it could be intuited there is a direction connection between H_3O_2 and The Intelligent Cosmic Vibration we discussed earlier.

Remember, the underlying composition of Agna (light), Yagna (fire), and Om/Aum. When these components are breathed into the body in the process of the Kriya Kundalini Pranayam extended meditative breath—in conjunction with the Sanskrit mantra, Om/Aum—it would seem at least plausible **we can create H3O2 through the light of the Sun interacting with body water and/or melanin and magnesium**... and use the vortexial/torus energies in the primal sound of Creation, Om/Aum—in place of water.

Certainly, these proceeding things become nails in the coffin of the Calorie Theory being the way the body sustains itself and as the only way to create fuel for the body. The implications of this added knowledge change the game and make Breathairianism more than some "airy, fairy theory" espoused only by delusional lunatics. In the face of facts and experience we can move the "delusional lunatic" moniker away from Breathairianism and into the mechanical theory of calorie metabolism, which has never been proven anyway— just a theory. So we could just stop our investigation into the feasibility of breathairian protocols; however, there are at least two more concepts to consider!

First, **in the process of performing Kriya Kundalini Pranayam(a) breath, there is an initiation of "The Intelligent Cosmic Vibration,"** chronicled in *The Bhavagad Gita,* which was previously discussed as Agna (light), Yagna (fire), and Aum (vibration). These three qualities all create energies and the electromagnetic energies could power a machine as well as a body, especially when there is an interaction with water or melanin, as previously discussed!

Regarding the second issue—**the soul is only energy, electromagnetic/light and fire in nature, and without a soul, no body can or will remain animated**! This is an interesting dichotomy... while the soul does not need the body, the body absolutely needs the Prana of the soul to continue as a viable entity! This was discussed earlier in this chapter, but I return to it again—considering the soul that is always being referred to is this pure Prana/Chi/light/fire electromagnetic energy, maybe it is easier to bridge the gap to applying this to the so called physical body. What is really being conveyed is the Intelligent Cosmic Vibration so frequently mentioned is the source that could power the soul so it can power the body! Am I leading you to a radical departure from the known and what is considered valid? Indeed I am, yet, nevertheless, **this vibration is important to seriously consider since it shows another plausible way a body can be powered without food!** This has not been scientifically proven through controlled tests, yet from observation, we know aura's exist around alive and thriving bodies, but they do not when those bodies expire/are dead. Anyone who has perfected their ability to see auras can validate this for himself or herself.

Note: *Everyone has this ability, whether they are aware of such or not. Even without the ability to see auras, we still have sufficient verification of this concept through Kirilian and Magnetic Field photography.*

Let's examine some other ways, beyond Kriya Kundalini Pranayam, of how we could increase the flow of the soul energy/Prana/Chi to the body itself and provide evidence of this occurring. Not to be redundant, but to reiterate one way to feel this energy, is via the Tai Chi "Standing Meditation" which was previously discussed and demonstrated earlier, herein. It is easy to feel this soul energy/Prana/Chi being magnified in the hands and face and body as heat and a tingling sensation. This noticeable transference of energy as heat and tingling naturally happens when **"The Standing Meditation"** is performed.

The same thing occurs in **Reiki Healing** as noted in a study by *Reiki News* by The International Reiki Center. Reiki practitioners' energies were measured with a magnetometer, which measures magnetic fields, showing quantifiable energy emitting from the hands of said practitioners. The same energies have been measured and seen emanating from the hands martial artists, especially Qi Gong practitioners, some of who can ignite newspaper and create a fire there from with nothing more than the energy from their hands.

Still another energy enhancing apparatus is available to us in the form of a pyramid. This topic will be thoroughly covered in the next chapter and the effectiveness of a pyramid increasing the power of persons, places and things will become self-evident.

Since the process of how using soul energy has been revealed, let's look at the ultimate connection to our objective: immortality. Soul-energy/Prana/Chi is comprised of atoms—and recall, as was discussed previously—these atoms never get tired, never wear out, and never can be destroyed, although their form can be changed but never extinguished. I propose then that in most cases, and maybe even all, we as individuals make the choice to separate our bodies from our souls. The decision for that separation may occur at the subconscious or unconscious level of human functioning... or it could even be reached deliberately if we begin to feel tired and/or run down and/or in significant enough pain we no longer want to remain on planet Earth.

Through my experiences, I know of at least four cases I feel qualify for consciously or unconsciously wanting to leave planet Earth due to the debilitation of a human body. One such example was my beloved wife, Charlette Ann Newton Smith, preceded by her brother, Jerry Smith. Another case is Judith Frankel and still another is my mother, Nadine Martha Newton Feldheim. I cite these examples only to substantiate I am not just making general claims but share this wisdom from personal knowledge and observation.

Robert J. Newton

***A person does not inherently have to leave their
bodies. It is something voluntary and not
caused or ordered by the Creator, God,
Intelligent Design, or the Devil.***

Agreed, there are some people who come to Earth for a
specific purpose and/or pre-determined span of time in which
they are incarnated here. Adding time, awareness and
understanding, I now understand and believe such designation
applies to my deceased wife, that will be shared in another
soon to be released book, *An Angel not Perceived.*

The passageway to an immortalized state has occurred in
myriad traditions and cultures, as noted below.

Kriya Kundalini Yoga: the personages of Babaji Nagaraj,
Mataji, Valmiki, Agastyar, Boganathur, Thirumoolar,
Rama Devar, and Konkanavar, et al. have gone into
Soruba Samadhi/immortality.

Hindu Tradition/ Krishna: Rama, Satchi Sai Baba, Sri
Aurobindo, Noga Baba.

Egypt: Thoth, Osirus and Horus.

Palestine: Jesus (Yeshua) and Enoch and Elisha.

Greece: Hermes Trismegustis

Central America: Quetzalcoatl.

The Middle Ages: St. Germaine.

Early England: Merlin.

Certainly there are probably other personages who have
immortalized their bodies as well but I am as of this writing
not aware of them.

Voluntary choice or not, the weight of the evidence is preponderant we can immortalize our bodies and in multiple ways and approaches. Fortunate we are to have these things! **Not all of us need to keep our chopsticks to remain in our bodies, ha-ha, but most of us will!** *Porqué*

| Chapter Seven

Are you ready for heaven, or in need of more leaven?
Quartz crystals, Pyramids and leyline vortexes might just provide such!

Some say you have to die to go to Heaven,

Yet that may be because they are without the leaven,

So when the leavening of knowledge and direction come,

We ultimately become more than the than the sum of none!

A pyramid is so very special, an uplifting form,

Most divine it is and can be even be worn,

Unrelenting in its power that can never be shorn,

Indeed its perfection derived from its divine atomic form!

Dr. Robert Newton, 11-04-15

NOW LET'S EXAMINE various forms and locations that bring more Soul Energy/Prana/Chi/Torus energies into a human body to aid in the quest for immortality. Leaven is a yeast and/or expanding agent that allows something to grow and increase beyond its original form and assume something grander. Something that works as a **"leavening agent" is the pyramid and the spire/steeple forms** found on many churches. More is documented about the power of the pyramid shape, but for the sake of a quick reference, note the spire form you find on Hindu and Christian temples; each has a similar effect to a pyramid as do the domes in some churches.

In the Case of a pyramid at the angle of the Great Pyramid in Giza Egypt, we have a Kirilian photograph—a technique of recording photographic images of coronal discharges that reveals the auras of living creatures—thereof, which indicates the energies referred to. You will notice in pictures about pyramids, **energy field photos are hauntingly similar to the double helix in our DNA**, which is often referred to as "Torus energy." What occurs here is not the pyramid creating the visible energy but acting as an attractor and amplifier, which ever you choose to view it:

Torus energy   *Atomic force*

Prana   *Electromagnetic*

Chi   *energy*

God life force

Orgone—an esoteric energy proposed by Wilhelm Reich.

Said energy experienced under a pyramid form is most intensely felt and infused into a body when a person is under the apex of the pyramid. Yet there is a residual effect that can be felt and measured even on the outside of the pyramid form.

Researching specific measurements relative to the Great Pyramid, we have the work of Joe Parr, an electrical engineer who completed fifty-five experiments measuring pyramids energies at the Great Pyramid, wherein he discovered said **pyramid energies can pass through objects.** He further discovered there is a bubble of energy that surrounds the pyramid, which certainly correlates with the Bosnian Pyramid of the Sun we will consider later in this chapter.

In the Great Pyramid, German scientists Born and Lortes found a double nine-amplitude energy in the microwave range above the normal nine-amplitude. Swedish scientist, Dr. Carl Benedicks found the same double nine-amplitude energy as Born and Lortes. They also recorded people inside the Great Pyramid exhibiting alpha and theta brainwaves. Both of these effects are significant to the ultimate purpose of immortalizing a human body!

Joseph Davidovits, in his studies and invention of geopolymer chemistry, on deeper examination determined the Great Pyramid is made from a synthetic geopolymer, mostly comprised of Calcite, a mineral which can resonate with the Pineal Gland in the head of the human body, and which has Calcite therein as well. Another Pyramid researcher, Doug Benjamin, mentions the Rose Granite that comprised the Kings Chamber of the Great Pyramid has the highest concentration of piezoelectric energy of any mineral. **This establishes the Great Pyramid as a substantial energy generator**; but its form/shape also attracts and amplifies Torus/Prana and the equivalents just mentioned. As a note: the mineral Tourmaline is considered to have the highest piezo-electric energy but undoubtedly, there is a high energy potential in Rose Quartz. Please refer to *Pathways to God: Experiencing the Energies of the Living God in Your Everyday Life* for more information about the energies in Quartz, Topaz, Tourmaline and other gemstones.

Considering the mounting evidence, I feel it fair to state what we have in this amazing Great Pyramid, as well as other pyramids, are substantial energies... far beyond those found in any normal distribution of energy of Earth. As Doug Benjamin, an energy researcher who investigated interior anomalies in the Cheops pyramid, has pointed out—**the Great Pyramid takes IR paramagnetic energy, which are induced magnetic fields that enlarge certain cosmic energies (Torus/Prana/Chi/electromagnetic).** We read of Sir W. Siemens, who went to the top of the Great Pyramid, wrapped a wine bottle with newspaper and collected static electricity inside his container. And in Christopher Dodd's book, *Pyramid Energy Generator,* we discover how the Great Pyramid was capable of, and in fact did at one time produce huge amounts of electricity as an energy generator.

Some scientists have conjectured the Great Pyramid was the model of a wireless electric generator, which Nikola Tesla created at his Wardenclyffe Tower. Former NASA scientist, Dr. Patrick Flanagan, who wrote the ground breaking book,

Pyramid Power, has measured not only large amounts of energy inside the Great Pyramid, but also discovered significant energy emanating from its five points (the four base corners and the apex/point). Due to the research of Worth Smith, in *Miracle of the Ages*, we know the **King's Chamber of the great pyramid is a scale model of the much smaller Ark of the Covenant, which has been conjectured to produce between five and seven hundred volts of electricity.** So obviously, if this is true, imagine how more energy the King's Chamber would have produced, due to its significantly larger size!

Now, let's take a few minutes and consider the amazing things a pyramid will do, including the ability to transmute gold to Ormus, also known as the "Philosopher's Stone. This topic will be covered more in a succeeding chapter, but we know from the preceding and following information in this chapter, **the benefits and effects from any pyramid form is the Yagna (fire) and Agna (light) factors that are absorbed by the human body.** The Greek word *pyros,* from which pyras or pyramid came from, means fire, and indicates the Greeks were acutely aware of this special power, and even more so were the Egyptians, Atlanteans, Mayans, and ancient Bosnians and Chinese.

The special power referenced relative to the life force of Yagna/fire/Prana/Chi/God includes a corresponding **shift into the higher functioning brainwaves in the Alpha and Theta range.** These brainwaves correspond with increased psychic abilities, higher creativity and better problem solving. So we are multi-benefitted by the pyramid form; this concept should also apply to a spire/steeple and even a dome. Now would be a good time to reiterate: "These alpha and theta brainwaves have already been shown to stimulate telomerase enzyme, the nectar of life, that keep the telomere in the chromosomes of the DNA from deteriorating and that keep our bodies from degenerating as well—at least in one aspect, if not all." So for our purposes, the telomerase enzyme factor is very important, even though every other benefit of the pyramid form is likewise beneficial for us.

This photo referenced as Fig.xxx reveals the Torus/DNA helix revealed by Kirilian photography

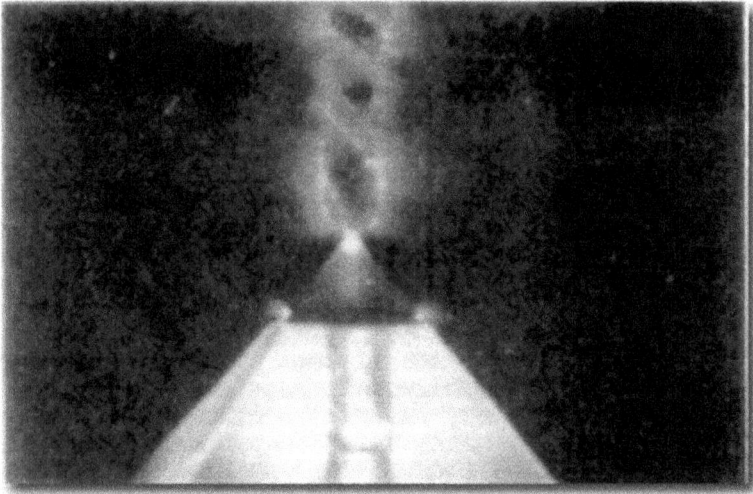

FIG# 14

Dr. Dee J. Nelson and his wife, Oso, produced this Kirilian photograph of pyramid energy using a Tesla coil in 1979.

A large pyramid is not necessary to focus and amplify Torus Energies, although as with most things in life, bigger is better. Yet a holographic eight-inch pyramid will work effectively to accomplish the task. Neither do we need an electrometer or a Kirilian camera to measure and quantify these things, since they can be measured with dowsing rods. If you are interested in securing Holographic pyramids, which are made from various metals, they are available from Pyradyne and Metaforms and other sources listed on my website: www.drrobertnewton.com/.

Moving on... not only do we have pure studies on pyramids but the measurable evidence, previously discussed, show the energy a pyramid generates is available, as well. Just looking at the preceding picture of the Torus energy, it is not difficult to see the power the pyramid energizes, in and of itself, and there is also a hint—actually really more than a hint—that our DNA manifests these same, or very similar, electromagnetic energy aspects. Since everything on planet Earth is energy, are we really looking at our DNA in its true form revealed in the picture? Beyond this, the following things were discovered by Dr. Andre Bovis, a French physicist and radiesthesist, related to the effects of pyramids.

First, **Dr. Bovis discovered a pyramid would vitalize body cells and even keep cells in the process of dying from expiring.** If this does not relate to the quest for immortality, probably nothing does. Bovis also found that plants in close proximity to a pyramid will grow better and seeds germinate faster and at a higher percentage than they normally do. Beyond this...

drinks taste better when put under a pyramid;

razor blades and knives get sharpened more easily;

batteries recharge more quickly; and

meditation is vastly easier to achieve and at a much deeper level

than without the pyramid energy effect. Beyond this, the severity of radiation was mitigated by pyramid energies. Each of these concepts are also covered more in depth in Dr. Patrick Flanagan's book, *Pyramid Power*.

In a Russian pyramid research project—wherein eight pyramids were constructed from fiberglass, up to 144 feet tall—an amazing amount of data shared by Dr. Alexander Golod, research director of this project. Not only is Golod's work a replication of what Dr. Bovis found, several other benefits of being in close proximity to pyramids were discovered: an **increased recovery from bacterial and viral afflictions, radiation mitigation, a lessening of weather and earthquake severity.** There was also a **higher concentration of negative ions** inside and outside of these pyramids. The significance of this discovery will be covered in Chapter Nine, and how very important this is in a quest for longevity/immortality.

Die Sonnen-Pyramide
Wärmebild
Normaler Hügel   Sonnenpyramide

Dr. Sulejman Redzic, of the faculty of Natural Sciences at the U. of Sarajevo, Bosnia Herzegovina, found the temperatures in the **ground around the Bosnian Pyramid of the Sun was five degrees Celsius higher surrounding the pyramid** than more distant soils. This temperature factor is cross verified by Mediterranean climate plants actually growing close the Pyramid of the Sun in the small geographic area around it. Janez Pelko, Bosnian pyramid researcher found the auras of eighty percent of the subjects in her study had **a significant increase in their auras** after just one hour in a tunnel connected to the Bosnian Pyramid of the Sun.

There are additional transformative issues related to the measurements of the Bosnian Pyramid of the Sun. The top of this pyramid was measured at **25,000 Bovis Units**, using an electromagnetic energy scale developed by Dr. Bovis, of electromagnetic energy. Further, inside the pyramid center near the top, the measurement is marked at 50,000 Bovis Units.

Now, and actually wow! The human body needs 6,500 Bovis Units to be reasonably healthy and 7,000 Bovis Units to be very healthy. So, in a life force/Prana sense and in a life extension and creating an immortal light body, what is going to happen when you meditate inside a pyramid? Even if you are using a small holographic **headgear pyramid, at the very worst you are going to have at least 10,000-14,000 Bovis units** of electromagnetic energy/Prana entering your body; and guess what?

On Dr. Bovis' magnetic scale, 10,000 Bovis Units indicate a power place on Earth such as you might find in the Bermuda Triangle or the Devils Triangle. At 14,000 Bovis Units, Bovis equates this to something ethereal, possibly akin to the energy that comes from the center of our Milky Way Galaxy. So if an immortal body of light were not ethereal, probably nothing on Earth would be, as well! Thus, the implications of using a pyramid to immortalize a body are of such amazing proportions as to be astonishing beyond all comprehension or close thereto! Question time? **"Does the power of a pyramid have the potential to change the form of a body to light?"** The most cogent response might be, **"How could it not?"**

Let's view some magnetic field photographs of the Bosnian Pyramid of the Sun and the magnetic effect on a human body. A picture is worth a thousand words and in this case, maybe a million or more. Physicist, Dr. Slobodan

Mizdrak, says these magnetic energy fields are vertical, which can be seen in images of the Bosnian Pyramid of the Sun.

Note: *There are actual magnetic field photographs that show the amazing energies either coming into and/or exiting the Bosnian Pyramid of the Sun, which are not shared, due to problems related to getting the appropriate permission to do so. Unfortunately, although there is some representation of the pyramid, this picture really does no justice to the immense amount of energies involved.*

Dr. Mizdrak has also measured an energy source buried beneath this pyramid at a depth of 1.8 miles. He does not indicate what this energy source is but I would conjecture and actually intuitively know it is a large quartz crystal such as is believed to be at the center of the Bermuda Triangle and The Devil's Triangle, among the other twelve-leyline intersection vortexes that will later be discussed in this chapter. In his research, Dr. Mizdrak also measured 10 Kilowatts of electricity being emitted from the top of this pyramid and found ultrasonic waves at 28 Kilohertz (KHz). If this does not reveal electromagnetic or Prana properties of the pyramid to you, most likely it would beneficial to go back and review the information in this chapter, so as to reabsorb and record what is being shared herein. Maybe the following will help in bringing a greater understanding of pyramid power.

Fig. 15 represents the magnetic energy field of a human body inside of the Bosnian Pyramid of the Sun.

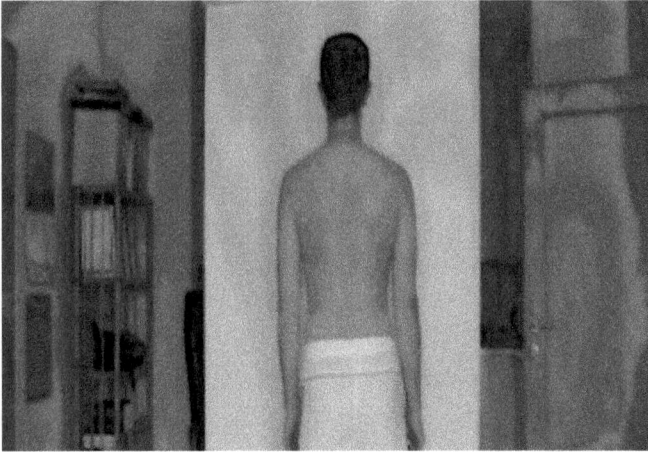

Once again, you are going to find the same magnetic fields in this human body as you find above the pyramid. These synchronicities or similarities reveal the kind of cross validation necessary to prove a higher significance of related energy fields.

Fig. 16, reveals auras from inside of the Bosnian Pyramid of the Sun. Again, you will see some huge and intense auric fields of electromagnetic/Pranic energy. The auric fields of subjects inside the Bosnian Pyramid of the Sun, displaying large and intense auras

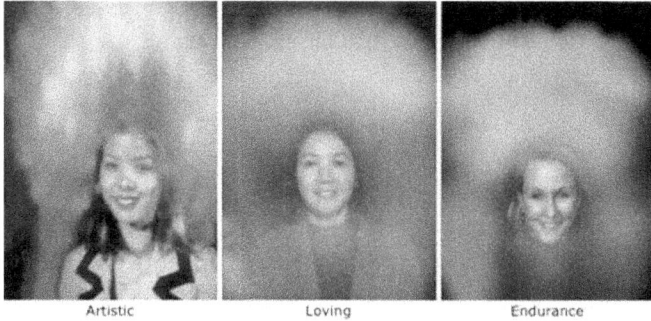

Artistic   Loving   Endurance

FIG #16

These magnetic field photos show auras at least twice what would be manifested outside of a pyramid form.

If we examine my image in Fig. 17, we are able to see an auric field which was captured just by using a headgear pyramid in conjunction with an engaging in a session of Kriya Kundalini Pranayam.

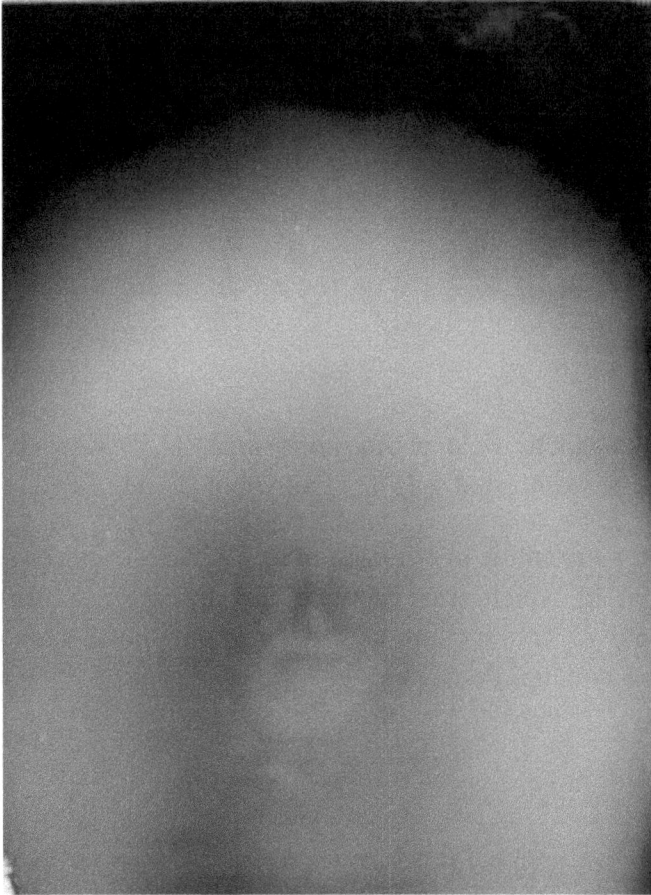

FIG #17

This is a picture from a Pranayam(a) session the author performed in 2014. Although this picture is not colorized, there is a large field of yellow prana topped by a band of blue light above that.

Another benefit about the pyramid that might surprise you is intensified sexual urges and orgasmic strength when people are under a pyramid and the influence there from. Any and animals will likewise gravitate toward a pyramid and the energies inside. When we collect all the circumstantial and direct evidence about the effects and power generated by pyramids, at the very worst, **exposing ourselves to pyramid energies will propel us in the direction of improving our health, extending our life spans, with the distinct possibility of immortalizing our bodies!** If we look to research completed on Russian pyramids, we find they generate generous amounts of energy even though made of a conductor of electricity, specifically fiberglass, which is far inferior to most metals and some types of stones like the granite, limestone and calcite used in the Egyptian pyramids.

A study in 2011 at The Norwegian University of Science and technology found people under a pyramid, even without meditating, are relaxed and wakeful and exhibit alpha and theta brainwaves. Again, it is the same brainwaves, which support the production of telomerase enzyme in the body that keeps the telomere in the chromosomes of the DNA healthy and radiant, and make us the same. So the telomerase enzyme has not been ignored but rather we simply have to set the foundation of the foregoing information to get to this connection to the telomerase enzyme. This could have just as easily been asserted yet it is preferable to build a foundation first and then the building, itself, thereafter, as it were!

The image in Fig. 18 is a 144 ft. tall fiberglass pyramid in Russia, constructed in 1990. Coincidentally, there is a Hertz (Hz) field resonance between the eleven Hz frequency found inside a pyramid form and the minerals quartz and granite, also resonating at eleven Hz. So, **if we hold a Quartz crystal in one hand, preferably the left one because it is the receptive, negative charge, there will be a more powerful effect on our Alpha/Theta brainwaves, and in our body atoms and cells.** If we hung a quartz crystal from the apex of a pyramid, it would add to this synchronous energy field. Atoms and cells are going to be more energized from the electromagnetic energies being combined and more energy leads to a less energy dense body... to a higher energy body of light and fire, wherein immortality resides. It should be further mentioned that according to some experts, the Great Pyramid in Giza, Egypt once had a quartz capstone of approximately nine feet in height,. Is that a coincidence? Considering what we know of the synchronous eleven Hz. Energy, such a question approaches a level of redundancy!

I have been told my Egyptologist, Larry Dean Hunter, there was no quartz capstone at the top of the Great Pyramid of

Giza. In my sessions of remote viewing, I have seen such so....

The aspect that makes quartz a highly energetic stone is the piezo-electric property, meaning it has a static electric charge. This property is what allows computer chips, which are silicon dioxide quartz, to store information in our computers and other memory devices. If we would substitute topaz for quartz, we would get an even more powerful piezo-electric mineral for use to increase the energy quotient in our bodies. Using tourmaline in place of quartz or topaz would yield even more energy potential and the bodily energy quotient increased even more. These principles are all highly detailed in *Pathways to God: Experiencing the Energies of the Living God in Your Everyday Life*.

If you do little more than meditate with these three minerals in your hands, you will enhance the energy or light factor possible in a person. If you combine these minerals, while being under a pyramid, you will magnify your energetic experience and brainwave levels into the realm of Theta. Combining these factors, by placing ourselves in a leyline intersection vortex, kicks things up to an even higher energy factor.

With the significant power of the pyramid, we look to yet another way to increase the energy therein, and that is through the use of applying magnets to the apex and corners as well as bisecting each base and side. The same process could be duplicated with quartz or topaz or Tourmaline crystals and/or pieces. The diagram seen in Fig. 19 will make this more understandable. Combining magnets and their paramagnetic fields with the piezoelectric minerals, such as quartz, will synergistically amplify all the benefits and effects from a pyramid structure.

Diagram:9
PLACEMENT OF MAGNETS & CRYSTALS ON A PYRAMID
APEX(TOP)QUARTZ CRYSTAL & / OR NEGATIVE POLARITY MAGNET
PYRAMID ANGLE
NEGATIVE POLARITY MAGNET &/OR QUARTZ CRYSTAL AT CORNERS
HUMAN HEAD
EYES
BROW CHAKRA
ALIGN A PYRAMID CORNER BETWEEN THE EYES SO THAT IT ALIGNS WITH BROW (FOREHEAD) CHAKRA.THE APEX ALIGNS WITH THE TOP OF THE HEAD.

FIG #19

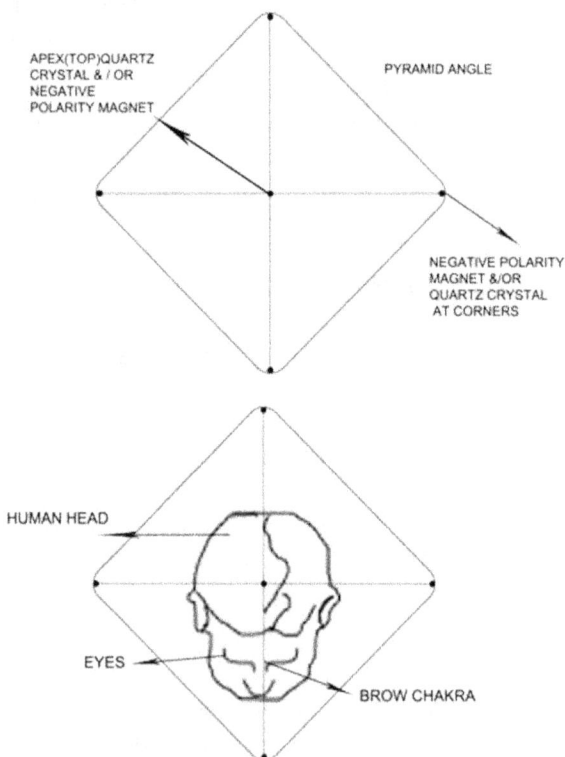

The diagram (Fig. 19) portrays a holographic eight-inch pyramid made from brass and can be coated with copper, silver and gold. It is usually worn on top of the head when meditating, studying, reading or whatever. The power of the pyramid can be more fully felt when one of the pyramid corners is aligned with the brow chakra in the middle of the forehead. A pyramid can also be hung from the ceiling in a room to dispense and disperse its energy there about. The Torus Field depicted in the Kirilian photograph of the pyramid, previously displayed, is a vortex... a torus energy.

Additionally, **it is important to note the angle of the pyramid sides will have more effect on some parts of the body than other parts.** Advanced information is available in both my previously referenced book, *Pathways to God: Experiencing the Energies of the Living God in Your Everyday Life,* and *The* Rosey Tablets, by Gandolph Slick, who is renowned for his teachings at The Temple of Sakkara. In each is a wealth of information directly related to the study of pyramids. You learn, for example, how the 52.5-degree pyramid angle of the "Great Pyramid" in Giza, Egypt, will strongly affect the heart of a person, opening it up and fostering a field of love. A pyramid with 59-degree angle will stimulate the hindbrain/medulla oblongata. A pyramid at 58 degrees stimulates the midbrain, including the pineal and pituitary glands. The pyramid of Khafre in Giza, Egypt, is 53+ degrees and The Russian fiberglass pyramids are even steeper than 59 degrees, which causes one to query, "Are they a cosmic antenna into the heavens and beyond?"

Robert J. Newton

Vortexes work in many ways similar to a pyramid and abound around the Earth including The Bermuda Triangle, The Devil's Triangle, and Lake Erie, as being the three most famous. There are twelve leyline vortex intersections, one of which is found at Four Corners, which marks the quadripoint in the Southwestern United States where Arizona, Colorado, New Mexico, and Utah meet. Drs. Olarinde, Olerud and Fuboya from the University of Texas at El Paso (UTEP), found a stronger gravitational field and electromagnetic force than in the surrounding areas. There are other powerful seven-ley line intersection vortexes in Sedona, Arizona, including Cathedral Rock, the Airport Vortex, Boynton Canyon and Bell Rock, among others.

Very deep meditations occur within these vortexes but more importantly, for our purposes, our bodies will be infused with more Torus, Prana, Chi, Life Force, or electromagnetic energies, spinning in a clockwise direction on the northern hemisphere and counter clockwise in the southern hemisphere. There is also the strong likelihood of our DNA being energized to a more highly potentiated state. The light and fire enhancing properties of these vortexes, as well as the shift of our consciousness into higher dimensions, has already been discussed but to address it again helps bind more of these concepts together.

Vortexes can be discovered or detected through the use of dowsing rods. At one point in my life, I was privileged to have two, seven-leyline intersection vortexes on my twelve acre farm in Virginia. This was unusual but many leyline intersection vortexes do exist throughout planet Earth.

118

It is also possible to create your own vortex through the use of large quartz or tourmaline crystals—the bigger the better. Large crystals attract the East to West and North to South electromagnetic leyline energies, using a large quartz crystal, and bending the lines as necessary to center on the crystal and begin to circulate around it, vortexally or torsionally with a Torus as a binary helix. The following shows how to find a leyline vortex.

Robert J. Newton

DOWSING FOR LEYLINES

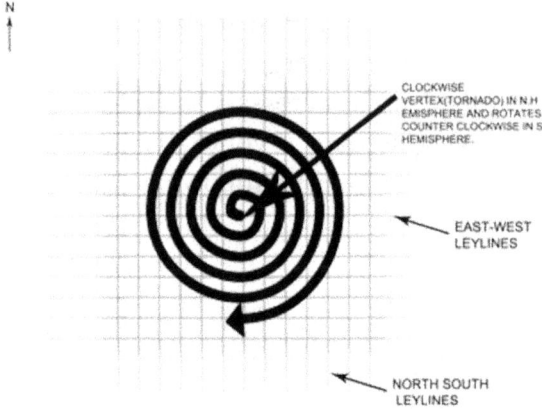

DIAGRAM #7

SEARCHPATTERN: DOWSER SEARCHES FOR LEYLINES IN A N-S & E-W DIRECTION AS YOU EN-COUNTER A LEYLINE, THE DOWS-ING RODS WILL PUSH APART.WHEN YOU ENTER A VORTEX,THE RODS SPIN CLOCK-WISE

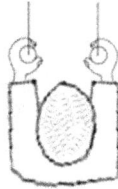

The human dowser holds the rods (not the dowel) parallel with the ground, arms outstretched and separated about shoulder width apart, hands facing each other but with the hand closed so that the dowsing rod can be grasped & op-erated.

TOP VIEW

A VORTEX OCCURS WHERE N-S & E-W LEYLINES INTERSECT. THE NATURE OF VORTEXES & LEYLINES IS E.M ENERGY/PRANA/CHI/LIFE FORCE.When Leylines are grouped (occur in mul-tiples), they will be at least several feet apart. Also, they do not localize but rather circumnavigate the Earth

FIG #20

The information presented in this image is explained in more detail in Pathways to God: Experiencing the Energies of the Living God in Your Everyday Life.

120

The energy inside these vortexes is often referred to as telluric energy and this equates to Prana, Chi, Torus, and Orgone, God-life force energies. So with this concentrated life force energy, **the more we are inside or near these vortexes, the more they will tend to infuse our bodies with Prana, Chi, and the electromagnetic properties of this telluric energy.** With this higher concentration of energies from the atoms that comprise our bodies, they will spin at a faster velocity and this begins to manifest the true energy essence of our bodies.

If, for instance, we perform a Kriya Kundalini Pranayam meditation in a vortex, we are going to attract a higher electromagnetic potential to our bodies. If we further combine this potential with a holographic pyramid over our heads when we meditate, and combine our actions with holding and/or wearing quartz, topaz and tourmaline, we increase the energy quotient of our bodies and they will be more light-like. It is in this state of light wherein we can exist in an immortalized body and the energy exposed in Kirilian and magnetic field photographs, as previously shared in this book.

Quartz resonating at 11 Hertz (Hz), which is an alpha range frequency in the brain/mind, has been mentioned in this chapter, as being conjunct, or in harmony with, the 11 Hz frequency of the pyramid form and as a way to attract and create a leyline-vortex intersection. It is the piezoelectric energy that is the inherent continual force that will attract and create a vortex, such as holding a quartz crystal in your hand, wearing one as a pendant on your chest, such as Dr. Fred Bell's Nuclear Receptor, or as a bracelet or ear rings on your body. This piezoelectric energy will be created more intensely by replacing quartz with topaz and even more so, by replacing topaz with tourmaline. So for those who seek the body immortal—those who need to get the atoms in their bodies spinning at a faster rate so as to shift their bodies into a higher dimension—wherein the body manifests more fully its true energy essence... quartz, topaz and Tourmaline should be seriously considered as a pathway to enhanced energies and a higher potentiated body... as in a light body.

The end result desired by so many is exactly why so much has been shared in this text, because when we avail ourselves to different modalities, there is a compounding factor, a multi-pronged approach if you will, that can only benefit us! There is little need to inquire what will happen when you use a holographic pyramid, in a leyline-vortex intersection, combined with quartz, topaz and/or tourmaline. The validation already exists—you will not be disappointed in the results of this combination if you are onboard with the premise of this book—and very possibly even if you are not! Not only will a body be manifested more as energy, the brain/mind will more easily transition into higher brainwaves and consciousness in the alpha, theta and delta Hertz levels. In the next chapter, the focus will be on other substances that can lift us into higher dimensions and create the alpha, theta and delta brainwaves that help create telomerase enzyme.

| Chapter Eight

Hallucinogenic, Psychedelic, Psychotropic Substances, Ormus and Finding the Body Great—Meaning—Preparing the Brain/Mind to Make the Climb to Bodily Immortality.

———————

When trying to enter the land unknown,
We can do this so don't bemoan,
You'll have found this as you've really grown
It is something more like a precious stone.
Dr. Robert Newton, 11-06-15

———————

So I am going to take a contra position to what I expressed in my second book, *A Map to Healing and Your Essential Divinity Through Theta Consciousness*. In Chapter One of this book, besides proving the existence of a Creator, God, or Controlling Intelligence, I stated that people who drink alcoholic beverages and/or regularly use Cannabis and hallucinogenic substances might never really know God in an unadulterated fashion. Such hard and fast rules were the result

123

of my wife and teacher, Charlette Newton Smith, who was opposed to the use of any mind-altering substance, influenced by her deep immersion into Kriya Kundalini Yoga and the Vedic sciences. She always did things through the ancient practice of meditation, which is embraced by large numbers of people today. There is a certainly validity to Charlette's viewpoint and yet there is a certain "blindness" to it as well. Nevertheless, I still honor her as my teacher, lover, best friend and soul mate, at a deep and mind blowing level!

Making my transition, **there are dopamine receptors in the brain that react to all of the substances we will be talking about, which are the same brainwaves in the Alpha/Theta range we create in meditation.** Many people have called these Cannabis or Dimethyltryptamine, a psychedelic compound of the tryptamine family (DMT), "receptors," yet that simply is not scientifically accurate, since these receptors will react to multiple substances and states of meditation.

Now, in the case of **alcoholic beverages**, they will make us feel good since they are **transiting our consciousness into an alpha brainwave range** and yet as far as immortalizing a body, this would be contraindicated since it so debilitates the liver and kidneys in the body—this puts the body in a toxic state where it most likely will not be able to produce enough telomerase enzyme due to the state of stress and inflammation it experiences from alcohol poisoning. I know this statement is not going to be popular, yet it is very true. So as it is true, it is! One glass of red wine a day is not going to ruin your life but letting go of this practice will keep your body closer to an alkalized state which is where a so called physical body and a body of energy and light reach their optimized state.

It does not take a lot of time to get buzzed via a meditation session rather than via a glass of red wine. Instead of "wine and dine," we could "meditate and dine!"

I am going to digress here, since I raised the subject of an **alkalized body being the optimal condition for us.** Alcohol, meats, poultry, fish, lentil beans, prunes and plums are highly acidic foods. Additionally, cooked meats, poultry and fish will not be digested in our intestines, because heating or cooking food kills the protease enzyme in them. This creates a condition where the intestines begin to collect and hold fecal matter, creating nitrosamines (found in beers also) and leading to the strong possibility of colon cancer, Crohn's Disease, diverticulitis, colitis and irritable bowel syndrome (IBS). Much better is a diet based on vegetables, potatoes, fruits, grains, rice, quinoa and beans rather than the meat and alcohol and diet sodas. Better yet, to transition to a breathairian type of living as such can be ascertained, if it is optimum for a person as determined by kinesiology muscle testing. Do not attempt this transition until someone trained in kinesiology muscle testing can ascertain what is best for you!

My discussions in this chapter may go against everything in current allopathic medical paradigm so **you will have to decide this issue for yourself. Dr. Newton is not going to make this decision for you!** But, too put things in perspective—let's go back to the Bovis units of energy we covered in the last chapter. **We know cooked food is not**

only going to be hard to digest, we also know it does not even produce enough energy to allow our bodies to thrive because the enzymes in the food are killed by the heat of cooking. In determining what is healthful for us and will highly power our bodies, there is only 1,500 Bovis units in cooked food and 3,000 Bovis units in steamed food—and we know we need 7,000 Bovis units to maintain maximum health. Sodas, at 1,000 Bovis units, will not only deplete our energy on the Bovis scale but will deplete our energy since the carbolic acid makes our bodies highly acidic. Raw vegetables will give you 6,500 Bovis units which shifts you to a healthy threshold: but even better would be eating sprouts, ripe fresh fruits, and nuts with 8,500 Bovis units and sunflower seeds, sprouted seeds and wheatgrass at 9,500 Bovis units.

Further consider, on this same matter, Dr. Robert O. Young's thirty years of research reveals a **body with an acidic Ph interferes with negative ions reacting with positive ions and releasing a bodily energy that transcends protein, fat and carbohydrates.** "The Ph balance of the blood stream is one of the most important biochemical balances in all of human body chemistry," states Dr. Young. He further states, "There is only one disease. And that disease if acidosis." Dr. Young's book, *New Biology,* explains this understanding in detail.

The importance of acidic balance cannot be minimized nor ignored because the negative ion factor has shown to be mood elevators and a factor in a healthy body. This will be discussed more in depth in Chapter Nine. **Neither can we**

ignore the breathairian approach to nitrifying the human body.

Ending the digression—we quickly return to the focus on hallucinogenic or psychotropic substances. Actually, Cannabis does have mind-altering properties as revealed in the study by Lukas, et.al, for the National Center for Biotechnology Information in 1995. **Brain tomography reveals alpha brainwaves are produced from the use of Cannabis and it functions ell as an anti depressant,** much better and much safer to wit, than Prozac, Ritalin and other related pharmaceuticals. However, if your desire is to immortalize your body or even take it an optimal level of health, you will need to have a constant supply of telomerase enzyme and you will need to be living more in a state of theta brainwaves to maximize this. Such might happen with Cannabis, but not as reliably as can be done in the deep breathing mediation of Kriya Kundalini Pranayam(a).

Two other issues with smoking Cannabis are bronchitis and emphysema, making it necessary if you are going to use Cannabis, to inhale it with a vaporizer and more optimally—with Cannabis oil.

One primary aspect about Cannabis that concerns me in regard to immortalizing your body is how the continual use of Cannabis could prevent you from reaching the states of deep meditation at theta and delta, and other activities that are going to stimulate more telomerase enzyme. One would seriously consider… if you already feel good, is there not less a compelling need or reason to meditate, especially including

Robert J. Newton

Kriya Kundalini Pranayam and deprive ourselves of unleashing more potential within us?

When we experience meditation without the use of Cannabis it is possible to see the dramatic difference something like yoga practices make in our life, giving us more impetus to pursue them since we know what our true baseline of consciousness really is. When Cannabis is incorporated into a daily routine, that critical distinction becomes much less apparent, as the higher brainwave level is obscured by the intervention of Cannabis!

In the case of using hallucinogens, psychotropics, and psychedelic substances such as Ayahuasca, Psilocybin Mushrooms, Peyote, Mescaline, MSMD (Ecstasy) and LSD—these will undoubtedly take you into the realms of alpha and theta brainwaves. The real question in regard to this issue is: **will using these substances have a long term effect in creating theta brainwaves or is it temporary?** In a study, *Effects of a Psychedelic, Tropical Tea, Ayahuasca on a Electroencephalographic (EEG) Activity on a Human Brain in a Shamanistic Study* by Erik Hoffmann, et al., 2001, it was found an increase in alpha and theta brainwaves in their study on participants after one Ayahuasca brew and more of the same brainwave activity after three servings. This still does not address if there is a permanent shift to alpha theta waves some time after these measurements.

However, successive sessions with Ayahuasca revealed there is a more permanent effect on brainwave modification into alpha and theta brainwaves and some gamma waves as

128

well. **So there can be a long-term alpha-theta shift in brainwaves and consciousness as well**. The question that needs to be asked, then, "How practical is it to continually ingest such substances versus continuing immediate accessibility to the Kriya Kundalini Pranayam(a) breathing meditation, that will do this reliably?"

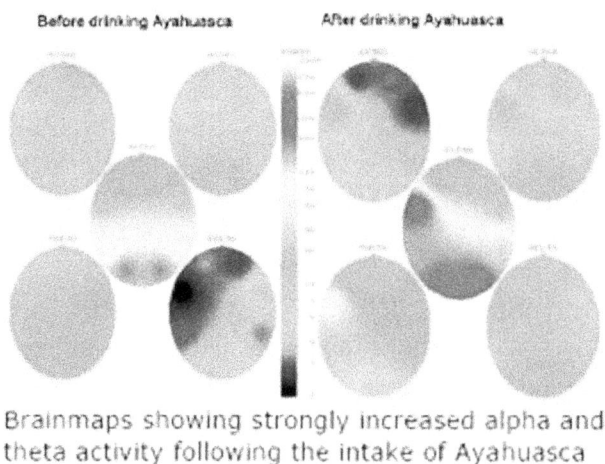

Brainmaps showing strongly increased alpha and theta activity following the intake of Ayahuasca

FIG #21

In Multidisciplinary Association for Psychedelic Studies by Wikler, 1954; Itil, 1968; and Frank in 1976 revealed information about LSD, mescaline, and Psilocybin Mushrooms and alpha-theta brainwave tomography, as well. R.I. Dafter's and E. Lynch's 1998 Thermoregulation study of MSMD (Ecstasy)[9] also revealed the same brainwaves present.

---

[9] http://thedea.org/docs/2005_Freedman_22686_1.pdf

Robert J. Newton

So how do all these psychedelic substances compare with Kriya Kundalini Pranayama and Kundalini Yoga? At first glance, it is evident they produce the alpha-theta brainwaves that eliminate stress and thus facilitate the production of telomerase enzyme. However, the **psychedelics do not appear to aid in bringing the Sun, Prana, Chi, God life force factor in the same quantities, which will infuse the body with more Agna and Yagna,** and the much-desired light and fire combination, as part of the Intelligent Cosmic Vibration.

This very important point many people using hallucinogenic substances will ignore, but ignored, hopefully this will not be!

In the deep breathing protocols of Kriya Kundalini Pranayam, you breathe in and hold hydrogen and oxygen in the human body. We have already established the alpha-theta brainwave benefits to these breathing protocols, but could there also be a combustion of sorts that occurs in the human body? **Can breathing power the human body into its true form of light and energy**, like the H_3O_2 created when sunlight interacts with water or melanin, in our bodies? It would seem—in light of the human body being able to take the energy/light of the Sun and interacting with the water in the human body to create a photosynthesis energy, H_3O_2— akin to what is routinely done by trees and plants... it could also occur **infusing humans with hydrogen and oxygen during Kriya Kundalini Yoga Pranayam(a) breathing meditation**. Does this establish and validate another connection, that being between Breathairianism, the cessation

130

of ingesting food and for some people, water, and immortality? This might have already been established.

Another thing that should be mentioned and questioned is whether DMT, the most prevalent active ingredient in Ayahuasca, is created within the human brain and in specific, the Pineal gland. This idea has been promoted by Dr. Strassman, who starting in 1984 has been exploring models for the DMT effect, re this matter; however, there still is no physical evidence at the time of this writing, although we know the Pineal gland does make melatonin, a relaxant and serotonin, a mood enhancer. Strassman also dubbed DMT the "spirit molecule" but centuries before, Rene Descartes stated the pineal gland is the "seat of the soul," which connects the mind with the body. We also know the pineal gland has an effect on how cocaine and Prozac create altered states of consciousness in humans. It is also known the pineal gland has rod and cones just like our exterior eyes and maybe that is why it has been called a "third eye," when associated with psychic sight and psychic abilities.

A very insightful book about Ayahuasca is Dr. Jeremy Narby's, *The Cosmic Serpent: DNA and the Origins of Knowledge*. This book shares in depth how Columbian Amazonian Indians use Ayahuasca to enter altered states of consciousness to get information used to heal people. It further reveals how these Indians decoded our DNA more than two centuries before our venerated scientists. Narby noted that Indians that looked forty and fifty years old were often actually in their nineties. It is hard to specifically attribute this healthy state to any one thing, but are the shifts of consciousness into the realm of theta, which stimulates more telomerase enzyme, responsible for it? In light of what has been covered herein and will be shared in later chapters, it is easier to answer in the affirmative.

Also, the Amazonian Indians shared with Dr. Narby the existence of mild hallucinogenic properties contained in tobacco. This information is most likely related to the nicotine we know to be in tobacco and would explain why cigarettes are so highly addictive; it is difficult to stop using something that makes you feel good!

Irrespective of the varying layers of knowledge, we know there are many other ways to elicit the alpha and theta brainwaves that are associated with the production of telomerase enzyme in the human body. This has been covered in previous chapters herein and will be covered in some succeeding chapters, as well. In the treatises referred to as *Corpus Hermeticum,* the following quote is attributed to Hermes Trismegistus, aka, Thoth, which is germane to our search for and implementation of our immortal bodies, "Focus your mind—I will teach you. You must understand that that which is within you, which sees and hears, is divine awareness itself and that the highest consciousness inside you is nothing other than Supreme Reality. There is no difference between your innermost being and God. Experience the light of your consciousness and realize what it really is. Those who remember their real nature attain the greatest good, knowing they come from a world of light, they return to that immortal light."

But those who prefer the life of the body become lost and confused and are subject to death, the Divine Shepherd explains. "Why have you surrendered to death, you men and women who are capable of immortality? Wake up! Stop your ignorant behavior, step out of the shadows and claim your birthright—everlasting divine awareness."

A few people will key into the most important parts of this message and those are, we are "capable of immortality," which comes from a "world of light," an "immortal light, which transcends the ingestion of hallucinogens." Remember, we already covered in Chapter Four how the word "light" is equivalent to the word "love."

The real key here, in Hermes words to us…
is just how much light and love can be infused
into our body and soul,
in our journey to immortality.

Actually, my experience with psychedelics is very limited, with only two Cannabis usages and yes, I did inhale, unlike the king of B.S., President Bill Clinton, ha-ha! Before I started practicing Kriya Kundalini Pranayam regularly, I experienced several Kundalini Awakening infusions that plunged me deeply into the fifth and sixth-dimensions or at least what seemed to be such, because that which is supposed to be material began to appear as energy, without clearly defined forms. One of these experiences came spontaneously; two others occurred on magnetic beds or pads and two more transpired with the Zygon—now Mind Tech—brain entrainment tapes. The first time I performed Kriya Kundalini Pranayam(a), I had another Kundalini Awakening as well as a concurrent experience of Samadhi. As far as I can tell from what people have related in their Ayahuasca, Psilocybin and LSD experiences, what I had was at least comparable, if not more intense and I have only heard of one person on Ayahuasca going into Samadhi, and even then only for a very short period of time.

As to how many people will follow my path, I will not venture and yet learning Kriya Kundalini Pranayam is most certainly the greatest blessing I have had in this entire incarnation. If it were not for my deceased wife, who was most insistent that I learn the powers of Kriya Kundalini Yoga, I might well have "missed the train" for this. There are listed two reputable sources where you can become initiated into Kriya Kundalini Pranayam. From this secret protocol, you will be commensurately filled with more light and fire factors infused into your body; you will not need the use of psychedelics. If you want only to get high and/or experience higher dimensions, as it were, and access more creativity, this will not matter as such for you; but if you want to inhabit a body of light, a Merkabah, you will most likely be benefitted from following my path. You are invited to learn Pranayam(a) from me by connecting at my website listed in the back of the book under Resources.

Next, let's move to an examination of Ormus, monatomic gold, which is not a considered a psychedelic, but certainly something that has a positive effect on the brain and the body. Unfortunately, to date, there has been very little research about this gaseous form of gold, called "White Powder Gold." This monatomic gold is in our atmosphere as well as other monatomic minerals and metals. The case for Ormus must be formulated from personal experiences and user testimony, since studies about this are scant, and relatively non-existent. There are many companies now selling an Ormus supplement and the question would be, "Why would or should this be used?" To answer that question we must go back into the historical times of the Anunaki/Sumerians on Earth.

We have records indicating there were people from the planet Nibiru/Mardoc/Planet "X" who inhabited planet Earth—probably as far back as 400,000-450,000 years ago; there is even the codex to their language on the side of a mountain or cliff in Iran. Based upon the codex, Zecharia Sitchin translated many stone tablets to give us a good picture of what these people from Nibiru, called Anunaki, really did and why there were here. One of Sitchin's books, *Including the Lost Planet*, details the Anunaki and their lives. From Sitchin's writings, we know these extra terrestrials used Ormus. Sitchin learned from his research that the people in *The Bible/The Torah* were in fact Anunaki and not Israelites. He writes of the Anunaki ingesting Ormus or monatomic gold-White God powder, for the express purpose its life extension properties.

We know gold structurally reveals itself as an octahedron on an atomic level and this same octahedron manifests in space in the form of exploded, red dwarf stars. There is no specific proof, extant, that Moses, Methuselah, or any personages known to have nine hundred plus year lifespans, actually ingested Ormus. Yet we know the Anunaki did so and they came to Earth in search of gold. So although it seems we can validate a longevity factor with Ormus, we cannot prove if there is a shift in consciousness into alpha and theta brainwaves when Ormus is ingested. There are many users of Ormus who will testify as to how it has slowed their aging, increased their intelligence, and altered their consciousness into the alpha-theta brainwave range, just not the kind of empirical proof we could really use, aside from the testimonials.

It is easy to create your own Ormus supply, by mixing an unrefined salt, like Celtic Sea Salt or Pink Himalayan Salt Crystals with oil, preferably high quality oil such as unrefined Olive oil. Ormus can also be created using a magnet with salt. As this is being written, the idea keeps repeating in my head about some major elements of Alchemy, being earth, air, fire, water, salt, lead and mercury. Somehow, someway, it is quite possible the Alchemists of the past such as Sir Francis Bacon, Roger Bacon and Sir Isaac Newton might well have known about using salt and oil to create gold, at least in the gaseous form of Ormus.

Do not be misled about the misperceted hype that the Alchemists were **only** trying to create physical gold from lead or Silver and/or Gold from Mercury. I am intuiting that Bacon and Newton were really searching for and attempting to manifest... the body immortal. I feel they were actually making Ormus. As to why this did not, in and of itself, take them into an immortalized body, possibly I should not conjecture, but I will anyway. **Ormus alone might not get you to the body immortal,** or so at least the evidence could reveal, **although extended life spans and improved health certainly are not beyond rational consideration.**

As this book was being composed, a relevant connection between pyramid energies and Ormus was revealed, through the research of Mary and Dean Hardy, authors of *Pyramid Energy: The Philosophy of God, the Science of Man*. They suspended a gold coin from beneath a small pyramid, and found it created an oily gold that is associated with the first stage of Ormus. Joshua Gulick, who claimed that a pyramid can make gold turn into a white powder, discovered the same phenomenon as the Hardy's, yet he takes us to a more complete explanation of a finished Ormus substance. Gulick contends Ormus is produced from metallic gold, which is then transformed into a white powder form, and that an even further refined Ormus can be converted into a red powder, known to Alchemists as "The Philosopher's Stone."

Putting merit in the research that goes before us, it should be noted that **just under the apex of a pyramid is the best place to produce Ormus.** As for other authorities on this Ormus topic, Barry Carter, the leading authority on Ormus, aka White Powder Gold, has been on The Dr. Robert J. Newton Show on The Artist First Radio Network, which is listed in the back of the book under Resources. On two separate occasions Carter shared his immense knowledge of the rejuvenating properties of Ormus and how to make it. Take heed, however, Ormus should be part of the immortality formula... not the only thing. If that were true, the writing of this book would be an exercise in redundancy. You can reach Barry Carter at bcarter@igc.com and whitegold-list@zz.net/.

There is no shortage of tools or techniques to aid our reaching the brainwave levels that will reduce stress and increase the production of telomerase enzyme and even HGH and ADT. From personal experience, something I find very helpful are the Mind Tech tapes I have used... previously known as the Zygon tapes. The new programs give you more cutting edge mind entrainment technologies that expand beyond just binaural beats and eye stimulation. There is also a brainwave entrainment device, the Mind Spa Mentor, which uses binaural beats and eye entrainment to elevate you to the upper levels of delta brainwaves.

Next, let's visit the "feel good" realm of negative ions.

| Chapter Nine

Negative Ions Can Make Us Feel Fine, Even When We Are in a Bind!

We know it takes more than a day to make wine,
It also takes more than a week to make it fine,
But with more patience it can be brought to fruition,
As part of our earthly payment of time and volition.
Dr. Robert J. Newton, 11-11-15

AN ION IS an atom that has gained or lost one or more electrons and takes a specific charge, either negative or positive, whereas a cation is an ion with net positive charge; it has more protons than electrons.

An excess of positive ions in the atmosphere make us irritable and depressed and make us more susceptible to sickness and disease because more serotonin is being created in the brain. **Negative ions in the atmosphere make us feel**

better, and boost our immune system, leading to improved health because dopamine is being created in our brains.

Obviously, we will always experience both negative and positive ions in the atmosphere but it is better for us if the negative ions predominate. Unfortunately, as a modern society, we are bombarded with air pollution and various electromagnetic waves from radio, television, cell phones and cell phone towers, computers, and microwaves, positive ions predominate in cities. Right now we have little control over the things above that lessen negative ions but there are ways around this.

Ways to effect—or regain a modicum of control over the influence of ions in our lives—include going into the mountains and desert as much as possible, especially spending time around waterfalls and rivers, which release a high concentration of negative ions. At the beach, the breaking waves of the ocean release a lot of negative ions, as well as the sand on the beach, which is silicon dioxide (quartz). Returning to the value of quartz, which we covered in Chapter Seven, I would have you recall the value of holding a quartz crystal in your hand or wearing a quartz pendant on your body to create your own mini-field of negative ions. The same thing happens if you wear a headgear holographic pyramid or meditate under a larger holographic pyramid. Even wearing a Nuclear Receptor, a pendant with a Solar Cross, or 144 mini pyramids will stimulate the desired negative ionic field, available at www.drrobertnewton.com.

The importance of integrating a high level of negative ions in our lives cannot be underestimated, as the following studies will indicate. Researchers, Goldstein and Levin, working under The Department of Medical Research located in Stahnsdorf, Germany, found **rats that had been deprived of negative ions had accelerated rates of death**, and exhibited neuro hormonal and Pituitary deficiencies. L. M. Livanova, et al., in a study at the Russian Academy of Sciences in Moscow found in their study that **negative ions protect the human body from induced physical stress**. Reilly and Stevenson, British researchers, at The Center for Sport and Exercise Sciences in Liverpool found **negative ions improved physiological states in humans, especially during rest.**

Studies at The Institute of Theoretical and Experimental Biophysics that were sponsored by the Russian Academy of Sciences in Pushchino, Russia, and conducted by the research team, Kosenko and Kaminsky, found increased antioxidant enzyme superoxide dismutase (SOD)—considered by many as our first line of immune defense in humans and in the production of small amounts of hydrogen peroxide. A higher oxygen content in the body, as manifested by hydrogen peroxide, would equate to more Prana, Chi, or light being carried into the body since oxygen seems to bond and perform as carrying agent for Prana, Chi, electricity, and hydrogen, as well.

Another study showed higher levels of Adeno triphosphate (ADT), definitely a life extension agent/body fuel and considered something that increases the light factor and energy in the cells in the human body, as discussed in Dr. Hurtak's book, *The Keys of Enoch*. In *The Secrets of an Alkalized Body: The New Science of Colloidal Biology,* by Annie Padden Jubb and David Jubb, it is discussed how electrons, light/photons nutrify the pineal gland, which was covered in the last chapter. There is no proof at this point in time that there is a negative ion connection here yet I have a strong intuitional hunch this is so. However, even if this particular connection does not exist, both of these things have a correlation to extended life spans and possibly immortality of the human body as well.

By not living of in a large metropolitan area and residing instead by the ocean or in the mountains or desert, we would give ourselves a huge advantage in the quest for immortality. I am sure most people will find this impractical; the vocation in which they are engaged makes the possibility impractical for the populace at large. At least, however, we can visit these areas frequently. Additionally, many devices have been shared to counteract an overpopulation of positive ions in our environments and create more negative ions. There are devices called "negative ion generators." They are made for homes, buildings, and even vehicles. Consider procuring these devices to increase your exposure to a field of negative ions.

I have to pause and consider, "What else can we do to stimulate the production of more negative ions in our personal human biosphere?" The Richway "Bio-mat" is filled with amethyst quartz and/or black tourmaline, both of which create far infrared waves and negative ions. For clarification:

"far infrared" is part of the spectrum of light emanating from the sun. It is not visible to the eye, but felt as heat penetrating into your skin. The quartz and tourmaline in the "Bio-mat" are more highly energized by an amplifying power source, or heating pad, which causes the emission of the "far infrared" waves and negative ions. This mat can be slept on or used in sessions. As well as the negative ion generation, the Bio-mat relieves pain. Further, doctors in Japan use this mat to cure cancer, as a thermography therapy, which reflects its power. These are available at http://drnewton.bio-mat.com

There are also infrared saunas that also produce negative ions, as well as remove toxins from the human body, and you will find Kriya Kundalini Pranayam and Kundalini Yoga not only produce the desired level of consciousness altering brainwaves in the alpha-theta range, but more dopamine and impactful negative ions are produced, as well. An increased negative ion factor is also manifested while doing Kriya Kundalini Pranayam, the Tai Chi "Standing Meditation" and Qui Gong.

Both Drs. Albert Paul Krueger[10] head of the Bacteriology Dept. at UC Berkeley and Felix Sulman[11], head of the Applied Pharmacology Dept. at Jerusalem University in separate studies and research, found negative ions create alpha brainwaves. **If we were to mix negative ions with meditation, where we also are creating these, we would easily be able to get into deeper theta brainwaves.**

---

[10] http://www.ncbi.nlm.nih.gov/pmc/articles/PMC2195229/pdf/879.pdf

[11] http://www.comtech-pcs.com/printable/details.html

Remember, the connection between alpha and theta brainwaves in relieving physical and emotional stress in the human body has been established. To mix the two allows us create a condition where the body is able to generate more telomerase enzyme... which then translates to the ability to transition to improved health, extended life spans, and the possibility of immortalizing our bodies.

Let us also reconsider the **power of the pyramid form to create negative ions.** Even if we are in a negative ion deprived metropolitan area, we can still choose to wear a headgear pyramid, meditate under a large pyramid, or use a nuclear receptor. Let us further apply the magnetic **negative ionic fields as being conducive to proper cell replication**, as well as factor in the increase of telomerase enzyme.

As I stated in the beginning of this book, referencing immortality, we are not "up the creek without a paddle." In increased knowledge and awareness, we become more learned in myriad ways, making an otherwise tremendous quest not quite so extreme—and very much within the realm of the doable! Let us not forget the words attributed to Thoth/Hermes in the Prologue of this book—many millennia ago in Egypt—where he indicates in *The Corpus Hermetica* that immortality is our right and this right is facilitated through the factor of light... literally how enlightened, enmeshed, surrounded and/or infused by and in light! I trust you notice how all that has been covered thus far is all interrelated is a most amazing synchronicity... a recognizable pattern, if you will.

*Stop for a moment and consider the many tools
we have at our disposal; it goes beyond just
mere coincidence.*

Preparing you for the next chapter... it is time to carefully examine the role of hydrogen and oxygen in the immortality equation.

| CHAPTER TEN

HYDROGEN AND OXYGEN – DO THESE RELATE TO PRANA AGAIN AND BREATHAIRIAN PROTOCOLS?

Hydrogen and oxygen, they are not just gases,
They could be more than something that fleeting passes,
*Could these **substances fuel** a body of light?*
Which becomes a vessel so brilliant and bright!
Dr. Robert J. Newton, 11-16-15

WE ARE GOING to reference a lot of what I initially covered in Chapter Six and some of it you will find redundant; the information fits well in Chapter Six, but most certainly applies here, as well. I deliver the messages in a slightly different manner so as to provide additional insights into the need for hydrogen and oxygen, as one way of becoming a body of light—a Merkabah—to enter an immortalized body. Another way to achieve the ultimate objective is through Soruba Samadhi, which may depend on the hydrogen/oxygen molecule of H_3O_2, aka, EZ-water although there seems to be no specific mention of this in Yogic or other texts.

Once again I lead you to a "land" virtually unknown in science—and rarely, if ever—considered even within deep esoteric knowledge, with the exception of the Egyptian priests and Thoth, who created *The Egyptian Book of the Dead*, and was hands on instructing these priests and the venerated Hermes/Thoth/Enoch. We are aware the Egyptian priests counterparts in India, known as the order of Kriya Kundalini Avatars and/or Satgurus, were likewise holders of this valuable knowledge. Kriya Kundalini Avatar, Patanjali— in *The Yoga Sutras*—and Krishna, shared it in *The Mahābhārata,* which we know to be one of the two major Sanskrit epics of ancient India and *The Bhagavad Gita*, a specific text extracted from the *Mahabharata*. In *A Map to Healing and Your Essential Divinity Through Theta Consciousness,*

I discussed how oxygen is used as a transporting agent to pull Prana/Chi through the blood stream and the human body. I hypothesized since the blood has negative (minus) and positive (plus) electrical charges in the blood, this process is made possible as electrical properties in Prana and Chi bond to the blood's plus and negative charges. I did not previously address the issue whether the positive and negative charges in the blood are infused from the Prana/Chi or whether the blood already had these charges and then attracts the Prana; yet it really does not matter—as long as the blood is the Prana carrying agent—which appears to be true.

*When we understand magnetism and it
predictable companion electricity, we likewise
understand electromagnetism.*

The positive and negative charges always look for
something to be attracted and bonded unto, as is the nature of
things in chemistry, and the molecules that are created from
single atoms that are combined with other atoms into
molecules.

After completing several years of research—especially
through an organization known as Mantle Dynamics founded
by Ronald Patrick Marriot, who documented a new energy
discovery from lightning—I am **certain there are massive
amounts of hydrogen breathed into the body, which serve
as a crucial function** in the process and has important effects
on it. One must see the certainty of the blood in a body as a
carrying agent for hydrogen and oxygen and Fig. 25
definitely indicates there is hydrogen in the blood, which
everyone seems to be ignoring, choosing to focus on oxygen,
alone. I am certain there is another type of a hydrogen/oxygen
transportation system. It is most likely related to the seven
major chakras, which we otherwise recognize as the energy
centers located at the root (base of the spine/genitals), the
sacral area (just below the navel), solar plexus (stomach
area), heart, throat, third eye (between the brows in the
middle of the forehead) and the crown (in the middle/center
of the head. Each is connected via the Sushumna nadi
(meridian), which is essentially a pathway of pranic/chi.

Robert J. Newton

FIG #22

The image symbolizes the seven major chakra energy storage portals, staring in the top of the head, delineated in white, and moving down to the root area, which if in color, would be represented in red.

As was covered in Chapter Six and reiterated again here, we have the process of H_3O_2 or EZ-water being created inside our bodies through a photosynthesis of sunlight and water and/or melanin (not melatonin), as related by Dr. Gerald Pollack, a professor of bioengineering who developed an explanation of water that has been called revolutionary. There exists another photosynthesis of sorts—**phosphorylation—a human photosynthesis that creates Adeno trio phosphate (ATP) and Adenosine-phosphate (ADP), and releases energy to power the body,** in contradistinction to the commonly accepted utilization of glycogen or glucose, which is believed by many chemists and biologists as to be the only way to fuel or power a body.

The following diagrams (Fig. 23 and Fig 24) explain how the phosphorylation occurs with glycogen or glucose, as *substrate-level phosphorylation*. The other, through *oxidative phosphorylation:* found in the creation of the body fuel as ADP and ATP. Oxidative phosphorylation is looked to as the process that makes the breathairian approach to not eating food—feasible. **Again, whether you choose engage in a process such as this is entirely up to you, the reader!** The concept remains far beyond interesting; medical experts and scientists who study cellular metabolism completely ignore and/or shun the reality of oxidative phosphorylation because it goes against everything they learned in college and medical school.

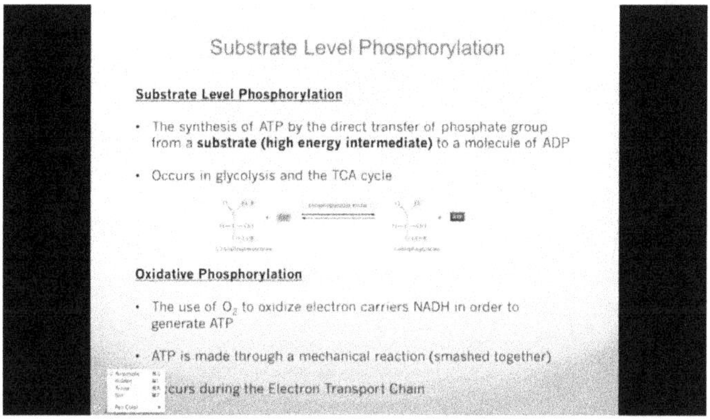

FIG #23

Note: *This image is attributed to Peter Cavnar – YouTube. In all due respect, we were not able to get permission to share* *the image, but choose to add the information here to support his extended value on the topic with the materials provided on his YouTube channel:*

https://www.youtube.com/channel/UCZLQkmBfdsU2bFzmm7lRI9g

As you might notice, the non-glycogen method of creating ATP through oxidation requires a lot of hydrogen and oxygen atoms, as well as a few of carbon. Coincidentally, we have each in abundance in H_3O_2, minus the carbon, which is well represented in the carbon dioxide we exhale. The following diagram, (Fig. 24) gives another perspective to consider:

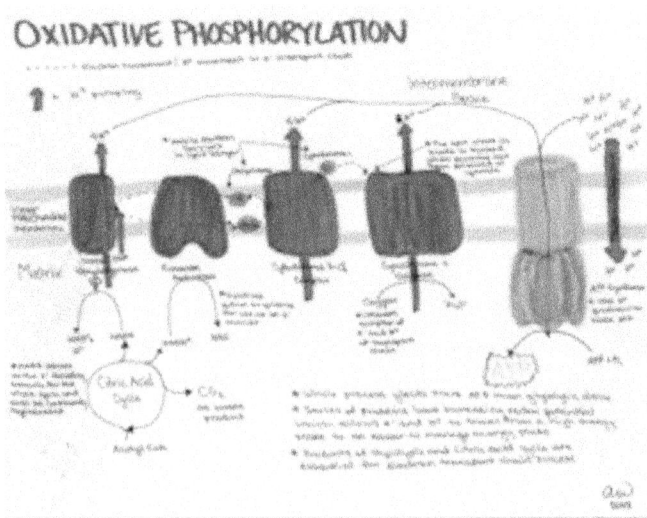

Note: *Image attribution at*:
https://www.pinterest.com/explore/oxidative-phosphorylation/

Again, we need hydrogen, oxygen, and carbon to provide the oxidative process necessary to create non-glycogen phosphorylation. ADP and ATP each has an affinity for hydrogen; it causes a type of combustion in the human body, via the oxidizing properties of oxygen but one might question, "Could this be sparkled by electricity from various sources, including the Sun, Prana, Chi, and/or melanin and catalyzed or ignited by the high-energy potential found in hydrogen?" As bizarre as many of these ideas may seem on the surface, they are probably no more on the fringe than the human photosynthesis of plants and trees. If you recall, there is already sufficient proof of that process, as was previously noted.

When hydrogen-oxygen combustion occurs inside the human body, it would most likely be a controlled reaction, since an explosion, which hydrogen has a propensity for, would probably cause irreparable harm to a human body **but not for a body that was in a state of light/light body/Merkabah**. As some scientific papers have postulated, the oxygen-partnered, molecularly bonded oxygen with the hydrogen in H_3O_2 probably modulates or controls the combustion of hydrogen.

Thus far, there is no proof this happens; there is no measurement for it, but in the land of alchemical reactions, we cannot summarily dismiss the idea either.

In fact, hydrogen and oxygen should be added to the traditional list of alchemical agents, fire, water, earth and air, as well as salt, mercury, and lead.

153

Robert J. Newton

Take note: hydrogen and oxygen are part of air, but never seem to be delineated as important elements of it. Is it then important that we stop and take time to question whether the hydrogen/oxygen connection is a missing part of ancient and modern alchemy?

Yet again, we have evidence of H_3O_2 and ADP and ADT as more than suitable body fuels... nutrifying without the glucose/glycogen that comes from food. Would you concur, this is what takes Breathairianism from a ridiculous theory, and closer to scientifically explainable? Remember, on top of this, the Calorie Theory is just that: a theory as of yet not proven as the way a body is fueled. **Is it plausible then to contend Calorie Theory really is more a fantasy than the Breathairian protocols?** The irony of this is most amusing, especially for me with all my years of study and research, and by now, hopefully, for every reader of this book, as well.

Addressing the engagement in Kriya Kundalini Pranayam, Kundalini Yoga, Tai Chi and Qigong, in which we inhale huge amounts of air into the solar plexus and/or lungs. Does this air not include oxygen, hydrogen, carbon... and the electricity or Prana found in the atmosphere on Earth? Can we conclude the delivery system for all these things already exists, as we just discussed? We are cognizant of the small amounts of hydrogen peroxide in the human body, so the question arises as to how hydrogen peroxide, comprised of oxygen and hydrogen (H_2O_2), gets inside our bodies. Is it perhaps made inside our bodies? We did address this topic in a few preceding paragraphs of this chapter, and question,

154

again, "Could it not be an intermediary step in the creation of H_3O_2?"

Beyond all that has thus far been mentioned, **we know hydrogen is necessary for an extended lifespan**, according to what we were able to glean from Dr. Patrick Flanagan, a scientist who worked on the Apollo Project and assigned the task to reduce the damaging effects of space travel on NASA astronauts. As Dr. Flanagan points out, **hydrogen protects a body from free radical damage, but as the amount of this naturally occurring element in our bodies decrease, the more we age and deteriorate!**[12] It appears to be time to question, What if we could replace the decreasing hydrogen in the body through Pranayam(a) breathing meditations, and thus reduce or eliminate free radical damage—and insure a continued supply of hydrogen to create the body fuel of ATP, without glucose/glycogen?

Now, the synchronicities start to descend upon as a study by Fahri Saatcioglu at the University of Oslo, reveals Sudarshan Kriya, related to Kriya Kundalini Pranayam(a), found the **deep breathing involved with this affected genes and lengthened telomere attached thereto.** It probably could not repeat too many times the benefits associated with Pranayam(a and Sudarshan Kriya.

This begs the question, "What about using existing supplements to achieve our objective?" I would reiterate said

---

[12] http://www.life-enthusiast.com/megahydrate-and-your-health-a-336.html

supplements, are made available by MJ Pangman and Melanie Evans under the same name as their published book, *Dancing with Waters*. Two key supplements are "Active H$_2$ and "Primo H$_2$. Both Pangman and Evans have completed a significant amount research into the rejuvenating properties of hydrogen, which these supplements have. Both biochemist, Tyler LeBaron, of the Molecular Hydrogen Institute, and Dr. Atsunori Nakao extol the virtues of **hydrogen to help people recover from chemo treatments and regenerate and energize a human body,** as many tests have validated. Intel Gadgets markets a Hydrogen Alkaline Water Pitcher that will infuse the body with alkalized hydrogen. At the worst, this should make us healthier, even if it does not push us toward immortalizing our bodies!

Fig. 25 reveals how hydrogen, carbon and oxygen react and bond in the human blood,: HCO$_3$.

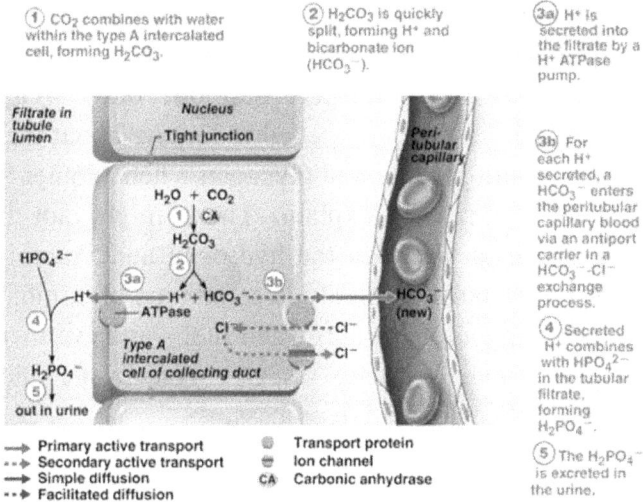

① CO_2 combines with water within the type A intercalated cell, forming H_2CO_3.

② H_2CO_3 is quickly split, forming H^+ and bicarbonate ion (HCO_3^-).

③a H^+ is secreted into the filtrate by a H^+ ATPase pump.

③b For each H^+ secreted, a HCO_3^- enters the peritubular capillary blood via an antiport carrier in a $HCO_3^- - Cl^-$ exchange process.

④ Secreted H^+ combines with HPO_4^{2-} in the tubular filtrate, forming $H_2PO_4^-$.

⑤ The $H_2PO_4^-$ is excreted in the urine.

Filtrate in tubule lumen

Nucleus

Tight junction

Peri-tubular capillary

$H_2O + CO_2$
① CA
H_2CO_3
②
HPO_4^{2-}
③a
$H^+ + HCO_3^-$
—ATPase
③b
HCO_3^- (new)
④
Cl^- — Cl^-
Type A intercalated cell of collecting duct
Cl^- — Cl^-
$H_2PO_4^-$
⑤
out in urine

→ Primary active transport
⊷ Transport protein
--→ Secondary active transport
⊕ Ion channel
→ Simple diffusion
CA Carbonic anhydrase
--→ Facilitated diffusion

FIG #25 Image Attribution: Pearson Education

So all the while you might have thought you were being taken on some fantasy excursion; nothing could be further from the truth. **While what is presented does not necessarily prove the combustion idea, where Prana/electricity combusts with hydrogen, it does validate hydrogen bonding with oxygen and carbon, in the phosphorylation process similar to H302.** It begins with H_2O, becoming H_3O_2 taking on an OH molecule reaching the H_3O_2 molecule, and operating in a very simple manner yet with sophisticated results.

All of this has been confirmed by the work of Albert-Szent-Gyorgyi, whose name you might recognize as a Hungarian- American physiologist honored with the Nobel Prize in Physiology in 1937. His work validates that **oxygen**

burns hydrogen—that is released into the human body as ADP and becomes ATP—in large amounts, every day, and amounts to approximately half our body weight in volume. Before you feel compelled to inquire about the need to use calories and glucose and glycogen when another fuel is at hand, let me further explain. There might not be an explosion going on between the hydrogen and Prana in our bodies, but there most assuredly is some type of combustion, of sorts... creating a lot of energy and fuel—and even without metabolizing food, glucose, or glycogen inside the our bodies—via a photo-oxidative process.

There is another important component: **the oxidation of hydrogen creating redox cells keep a body regenerated.** Redox cells are very particular to our quest and fortunately can be supplemented into a human body through a redox supplement developed and distributed through ASEA, LLC—a privately owned company, which was previously known as Medical Immune Research, Inc., and founded in 2007. I have not noticed a huge difference in my health and body functions from using ASEA products, yet there may be subtle changes occurring.

Among the issues to be discussed under this chapter's topic is another process that makes the breathairian approach to living and immortality feasible. Let's discuss the close similarity to the information in the last two or three pages herein and in Chapter Six—for the specific reason to look at the same concepts from as many angles as is possible from the foundation of our previous discoveries. I am sure you fully understand we are on the frontier of human body metabolism and a more important goal: immortalize a human body.

The **"fourth phase"** of water is not in a free state; **it is structured**, in a hexagonal lattice within the surrounding water. Individual H_2O molecules form loose ionic bonds creating an H_3O_2 lattice. **This water is found intracellularly and essential for all life processes,** which is the evidence proving the efficacy of structured water, juicing and urine therapy.

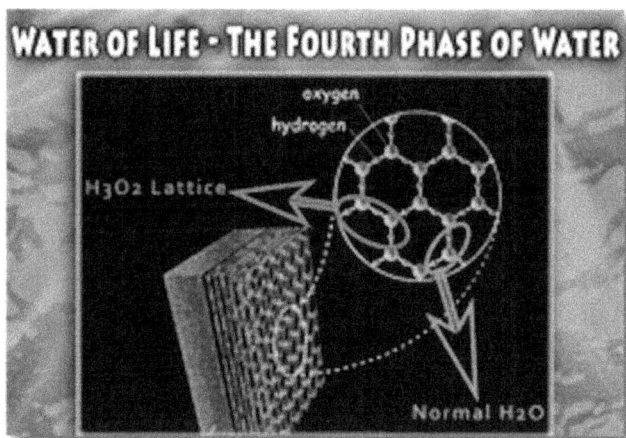

FIG #26

H_3O_2, a state of water which can be called structured, is extremely pure, and accessible to the body. The image more accurately displays how the H_3O_2 or EZ-water is created, but it does omit a possible intermediary state of H_2O_2.

Photo Attribution: http://sitsshow.blogspot.com

Especially in the **Kriya Kundalini Pranayam(a) breath**, which is extremely extended in nature, truly **we bring and hold more hydrogen and oxygen into the body**, than any other meditation or breathing protocol we have access to. Would this make Kriya Kundalini Pranayam an essential component of our quest to immortality? I would contend the answer is an unquestioned, "Yes; that it could have the same effect as sunlight in creating H_3O_2? The things we have covered certainly seem to hint at such—and at worst would still be health enhancing and have life extension components. Is this exciting and relevant to our quest? If you are just reaching a level of awareness about how hydrogen and oxygen react inside the body—and in light of this reality—I am confident you share my excitement that things are "lining up" for us... and probably far more than most scientists in cellular biology or chemistry would have thought we could discover or be able to ascertain!

Much of what has been shared with you to this point was designed to help you eliminate any physical obstacles to immortalizing your body. However, I know of one obstacle remaining in our path. It is significant enough to warrant it's own chapter, as we examine how we are being trapped into reincarnating on Earth—through the improper dispensation of the concept of karma.

CHAPTER ELEVEN

GETTING OFF THE WHEEL OF KARMA AND NEAR DEATH EXPERIENCES. HOW LONG DOES IT TAKE BEFORE WE GO TO HEAVEN?

———◇◇◇———

Pardon me but my kar(ma) has just run over your dog(ma).

So why would you want to run over my dog(ma) since he is really a hog(ma)?

So what if my hog(ma) told you your dog(ma) that your kar(ma) was holding you back?

Would you really think me a clueless jokester… a most deluded hack?

Dr. Robert J. Newton 11-25-15

———◇◇◇———

CHRISTIANS, MUSLIMS, AND Jews almost universally believe the "one and done" concept to our lives here on Earth. This is because texts and teachings about these things have been edited and reincarnation is dismissed as ranting and a deluded notion. Yet in *Reincarnation: The Phoenix Fire Mystery,* author, Sylvia Cranston, reveals how reincarnation is or was a part of all religions and almost all philosophies. At the very least, we see the phenomenon of reincarnation in the accounts of myriad people relating their experiences in "near death" experiences or occurrences (NDE's). Many neurologists have dismissed NDE's as a fantasy or dream; the result of a chemical reaction in a dying brain. However, there is one neurologist—a famous brain surgeon—who came to believe otherwise. Dr. Eben Alexander, III is a renowned American neurosurgeon author of *Proof of Heaven: A Neurosurgeon's Journey into the Afterlife*. Alexander pragmatically describes his 2008 near-death experience and avows science can and will determine heaven does exist. At one point in life, Alexander did not believe in God or reincarnation, nor did he believe there was validity to other people's accounts of their own NDE's. One can only imagine the experience and transformation that led to his subsequently writing *Proof of Heaven*, after his own NDE and the follow-up, *A Map of Heaven*, where he takes a much broader view—in his quest to deliver a message of how modern science is on the verge of the most profound revolution in recorded history.

With no intention to ruin the telling of the story for you, but to summarize sufficiently to piqué your interest, I want to share what happened to Dr. Alexander. Essentially, he died from bacterial meningitis of the brain, wherein there was a significant edema and a consequent swelling, which resulted in a flat-lined brainwave/death. Alexander was later able to recount—in detail—the procedures and surgeries performed on him by the neuro surgeons trying to resuscitate him. After he recovered from his "death," Dr. Alexander recounted what the surgeons had done to his body and also how there was in fact a heaven.

Not only does not everyone have this opportunity, but Dr. Alexander's personal experience correlated with the research completed by Drs. Raymond Moody Thelma Moss on people who had NDE'S and were able to relate their death experiences. There is a haunting similarity to these accounts, in such high numbers, one comes away with more than finding them interesting: **a belief is formed that this type of reincarnation simply cannot be ignored—nor can be dismissed** except by skeptics who are "dead set" against the continuation of the soul and monad, which were comprised in the Theosophical and Vedic (Indian) traditions.

There is an archive of Dr. Alexander's interview on "The Dr. Robert J. Newton Show on "The Artist First Radio Network," as noted in the Resource section in the back of the book.

There is no doubt Hindus, Yogis, Taoists and Buddhists completely accept reincarnation; it is never questioned, but I do question is **whether we need around 2000 incarnations to get off the proverbial "Wheel of Karma" to manifest our body of light or Merkabah** before we can transition into a state of immortality? A deep and probing question... this, yet the two thousand life-time requirement—or curse if you will—is generally accepted without much protestation by the above religions and philosophies, and was mentioned by my teacher in Kriya Kundalini Yogi, Govindan Satchidananda, many times. Yet we must look deeper to understand just why the 2000 lifetime requirement is so firmly entrenched in Yoga, Hinduism, Taoism and Buddhism.

Let's consider that *In The 72 Names of God: Technology for the Soul*. Rabbi Yehuda Berg proclaims we are already perfect but we come to Earth to play a "game" in which the knowledge of our perfection is wiped from our memory and our goal in this "game" is to search out and re-find our perfection. This is expressed in the Seventh Name of God, "Aleph Kaf Aleph," which in Hebrew means, perfection or restoring things to their perfect state.

Note: *The preceding is attributed to Rabbi Berg, which is something I read in the past and remembered. Please understand it is not a direct quote.*

Karma and the pursuit of perfection serve well to lead us to the inevitable question, **"If we are already perfect and we are only playing a game t rediscover this perfection, why would we be chained to having at least two thousand lifetimes to discover and/or uncover the inherent perfection, we already possess?"** The Hindu answer to that would be Karma, but really, what is Karma? *The Spiritual Encyclopedia* reveals "karma" as a Sanskrit word that means: "act," "action," and "word." It further relates Karma as a chain of words and actions, which create a cause and affect we then experience, and states it is a process, designed for our good, which allows us to perfect ourselves and remove our flaws.

We must now pause and consider more deeply both "Aleph Kaf Aleph," which tells us we are already perfect;

Jesus' *Sermon on the Mount,* where he shared, "Be perfect, therefore, as your heavenly father is perfect;" and the Vedic or Indian concept of Maya that would convince us imperfection is nothing more than a powerful illusion. I ask you then, "How confused—how unperceptive—would we have to be to need 2000 life times and maybe 100,000-140,000 years of living to figure this out?"

Now, let's pursue this deeper, considering Sir Isaac Newton's work in *Philosophiae Naturalis Principia Mathematica, The Third Law of Motion,* which simply states that for every action there is an equal and opposite reaction. Newton's theory is prescient for our purposes since it does not suggest a delayed reaction to an action, such as that mentioned in *The Spiritual Encyclopedia.*

What is revealed is: the reaction to our actions is not delayed and karma does not hang around necks like an albatross, as long we deal with things as they occur and not sweep them under the rug. We might even be able to proclaim it is not possible to sweep things under "the rug" since there is no delayed effect and consequences that would violate the laws of physics and even chemistry!

The implications of this discussion are huge because **we can get off The Wheel of Karma, much sooner than is universally believed!** Could this idea of being trapped on this proverbial wheel be an ecclesiastical maneuver to keep us enmeshed in a religion, whereby we contribute money to gain some type of dispensation from the actions of our sins?" I say in all honesty, "I used to believe the two-thousand lifetime karma conundrum, but there is nothing that proves such and Newton's *Third Law of Motion* brought the idea into greater question, so I suggest we question it—in a loud fashion!" In expressing such, I do not condone nor advocate that we are not charitable and equitable in our actions toward people and animals and even our Earth. In the end however, people experience the things in their lives they create, irrespective of their actions being enacted consciously, subconsciously, or unconsciously.

We have to let go of blaming other people, sources, and God or the Devil for our woes; these things land squarely upon our own feet/feats, as it were!

Additionally, if we live our lives by *The Golden Rule* whereby we have been taught to "Do unto others as you have them do unto you," we can smooth the path to immortality, jump off that nasty Wheel of Karma, and attain a state of bliss, no longer subject... "to suffer the slings and arrows of outrageous fortune," as mentioned in William Shakespeare's, *Hamlet* and an annoying and disabled deteriorating body!

You really can get off the hamster—and human—treadmill! Join with me as we courageously circumvent the plethora of myths and distortions about karma—and claim our right to immortality. Notice, in *The Sermon on the Mount,* Jesus does not mention atoning for our past actions... only us being perfect as is our heavenly Father.

There has been a broad base of material covered, calling for a summary of sorts, which be appropriate to bring about the level of cohesive understanding that makes sense of the varied elements presented—would you agree or do we need a forum of three?

| CHAPTER TWELVE

INTO A SUMMARY WE SHALL DELVE.

In a summary we shall investigate,
If we have missed anything we can mitigate,
If there is anything that is remiss,
We can probe it and not dismiss!
Dr. Robert J. Newton, 3-7-16

IN ALL MY books, be they fiction or non-fiction, I push myself into new territories of knowledge and information— daily, hourly and minute-by-minute. So much information has been covered... beyond my fiction look at immortality, in which I covered a lot actual things about immortality in a previous book, *In Search of the Body Immortal: Let the Journey Begin.* Even I am amazed some of the nooks, corners and crevices from which this information has come— especially those roused through intuitional hunches: information from the Akashic Records as were loosely translated as knowledge from the skies/universal computer,

Celestial Hearing considered a universal hearing of knowledge from Patanjali's *The Yoga Sutras*), "The Cosmic Computer" referenced in Dr. Hurtak's *The Keys of Enoch*, and inter dimensional knowledge from remote viewing (a mind excursion into other dimensions).

Chapter One: We discover the ways in which we become ill, degenerate and trail off into death. These states stem from the telomere in the chromosomes in the DNA, as it begins to unravel and create incorrect duplications of cells and/or stop replicating cells altogether. Certainly there must be emotional and mental components that cause this malfunctioning in the telomere and in fact stress has been identified as a major cause in the degeneration of telomeres discussed in the next chapter. We also found ways to increase our functioning through using precursors' of human growth hormone (HGH) through the amino acids of arginine, glycine and glutamine. We also discovered how hydrogen rich supplements will counteract aspects of oxidative stress.

Then we discovered how emotions, mind programming and supplements could stimulate the telomerase enzyme to keep our telomere functioning optimally. Additionally, there is an established direct link between our dominant brainwaves and our state of telomere health, with Alpha brainwaves (somewhat) and Theta brainwaves (even more), which put us in a position to stimulate elevated levels of telomerase enzyme. We also discussed the many supplements, herbs, vitamins, minerals, amino acids and enzymes that promote the production of telomerase enzyme.

Chapter Two: The intent was to increase awareness of other causes of aging, including glycation and oxidative stress, which are caused when glucose sugar binds to our DNA, proteins and lipids. Hydroxyl radicals also cause oxidative stress. Additionally, stress in general not only causes sickness and disease but also stops the generation of telomerase enzyme inside the body, thus setting the stage for telomere degeneration and then problems with cell division or even a cessation thereof. However, through the use of mind re-programming via Neuro Linguistic Programming, Silva Mind Control and Theta Consciousness Reprogramming, we can negate the negative programs responsible for making us sick, degenerate, and die—even the physical factors that cause this. Beyond this, we absorbed the awareness of how atoms that comprise the cells never wear out and/or malfunction!

It was further revealed we have been programmed to get sick, degenerate and die, which has come through various institutions on Earth, be they schools, governments, religions, allopathic medicine or corporations. Most of this is done in a propaganda campaign—in an attempt to convince us of something not fundamentally true—although the veracity of the inevitability of death is universally accepted.

Next we ventured into the perfect nine geometric forms of all creation—and the foundation of all things on a human level and beyond—and how these forms are repeatedly replicated as per Valery P. Kondratov's, *Geometry of a Uniform Field*. What we discovered is a perfect structure and perfect atoms on the atomic level of creation, the building blocks of everything; guiding us to exhibit similar

171

characteristics of perfection. We also found perfect cymatic or vibrational waves from the "Primal Sound" of Om/Aum and the perfection expressed through "The Intelligent Cosmic Vibration" from *The Bhagavad Gita* composed of Om/Aum, Yagna (fire) and Agna (light). All of which is further evidence we do not live in a Universe of dense matter but rather vibration and light, which are inherently non-material and fundamentally energy.

Time was spent assessing various mind re-programming techniques; the performance of which can put our minds in a receptive state to accept the reality of being able to live without sickness, degeneration and death. We discussed the types of meditation which stimulate telomerase enzyme including:

Qui Gong;

The Tai Chi Standing Meditation;

Kriya Kundalini Pranayam(a) breathing meditation;

The breathless state of Samadhi;

The "Aum/Om" mantra;

The Gayatri Mantra;

The Maha Mrityunjaya Mantra, and

The 72 Names of God, from "Exodus" of The Torah.

No study would be complete without addressing the feelings of love, including kissing, sexual union and more, as telomerase enzyme stimulators. The chapter focused on other telomerase catalysts found under or around a pyramid, leyline vortexes, structured water, Yoga Asanas and other stretching,

172

exercise, dancing, singing, laughing, sports and extreme sports. We found inheriting DNA that has more telomerase enzyme capabilities, as do Ashkenazi Jews, is quite propitious, as well.

Additionally, we looked to sexual activity, especially orgasm, to create theta brainwaves and we found them associated with stimulating telomerase enzyme. The intent was not to ask you embrace a "one trick pony" but rather provide you with multiple ways to stimulate telomerase enzymes. My experience—my life path the last thirty-six years—has been this multi-disciplinary approach to increased awareness. Since changing to this operating system, as such, I have learned faster and made realizations most likely not made from a mono disciplinary approach!

Validation of an interesting connection between exercise, sports, dancing, stretching and yoga came from understanding the movement involved in all of these. There has been more than one famous Yogi, who could perform miracle like things and yet once they stopped engaging in the Yoga Asanas (stretching), their bodies began to deteriorate rather quickly, soon followed by death. Please, please, please, take this to heart and realize some type of at least moderate exercise is necessary to remain vibrant and vital! As an extension, this concept applies to immortalizing a body into a realized body of light. Remember, short intense bursts of exercise or long stretching sessions give us the highest benefit from our exercise.

Robert J. Newton

Additionally, we covered how alchemy works and the finer aspects of the topic, as was uncovered in Dr. Paul Foster Case's "Builders of the Adytum" lessons. It was further discussed how the alchemists of the past might have been searching to make the monatomic form of gold, Ormus, a gaseous "white gold" that is known to have health, mental and life extension benefitting properties. Later, in Chapters Six and Ten we discovered the alchemists may have also been using hydrogen, oxygen and even carbon to assist the human body to create H_3O_2 and the process of oxidative phosphorylation, where the body fuel of Adeno triphosphate is created—without food and the glucose and glycogen that come there from.

The importance of deep relaxation as it applies to filling the body space with more Prana/Chi/light/fire/God life force was examined, in relation to allowing the brain to access and function at higher levels of alpha and theta brainwaves. The specific benefits we get from this level of relaxation are a more vitalized body, longer life spans and the stimulation of telomerase enzyme, not to mention functioning with higher intelligence and creativity. To reiterate this deep relaxation comes from deep meditation, especially Kriya Kundalini Pranayam, the Tai Chi "Standing Meditation" and "The Backflow Meditation." A strange dichotomy it would seem to find the same deep relaxation found in meditation to also be found in deep sexual orgasms, singing, playing music, competitive sports and extreme sports such as surfing, skiing, snowboarding, motocross, and sky diving.

174

Chapter Three: We discovered the magnificence of trees, how they should be respected, how we cannot live without them—and even that they know they need to sing to remain healthy and balanced. We further discussed the consciousness altering properties of the Sanskrit mantras of Aum, Gayatri, and Mahamrityonjaya—and how the alpha and theta brainwaves produced therefrom help us to produce more telomerase enzyme. A degree of focus was placed on how both Sanskrit and Hebrew and cymatic/vibrational properties balance our emotions and transport our bodies to a point of existing with more light, and less dense matter, which is really dense energy.

We also covered how our bodies and minds are commensurately benefitted from certain sounds from the Solfeggio frequencies/scale, specifically 528 Hz and the correlation to 432 Hz of the diatonic frequencies/scale and the Shuman Earth Resonance of 7.83 Hz and oscillations above the 7.83 base rate. If you recall, this reveals a series of parallel synchronicities that are much more powerful when combined than when separate. The point being revealed is how certain distinct sounds will tune our bodies to a higher frequency, emitting more Agna (light) and moving our brain-mind into the alpha–theta brainwaves that give us the insight and power to direct and use these frequencies/sounds to an ascended light body... an immortal merkabah.

Chapter Four: Interestingly, we viewed how words are inherently ambiguous, high level abstractions; necessitating us to delve into the realm of numbers so as to gain more insight and direction to the path of immortality. We learned the word immortality equals 101, which equates to God force, infinity, spiritual knowledge, personal development and universal energies. All of these are qualities that are essential/necessary to a clear path on the road to immortality. Deconstructing to the point of best understanding and clarity, the number 1 equals God force, initiative, and inspiration. The number 0 equates to eternity, enhancing spiritual abilities, and developing intuition. Each will push us along our path of the Merkabah, which if you didn't catch this in earlier chapters, is an early Jewish practice concentrated on visions such as those found in the Book of Ezekiel Chapter 1, or in other literature of the time, concerning stories of ascending to the heavenly palaces and the Throne of God. Finally... reviewing vital information about 101 equaling 2, which happens to be an angel number; knowing this is not just an academic exercise, but rather gives us insight into how we would contact and be directed by angels.

The important thing about numbers is not only the clarification they give to words and their equivalents, but being something we actively use and entertain in our thoughts to push closer to the light of immortality. There was also the consideration to change our names to ensure they equal the particular numbers that put us in a sympathetic vibration with what we want to manifest—crafting a name that equals 101 would most assuredly aid us in a pursuit of immortality.

Chapter Five: I hope you enjoyed the discussion of angels; specifically the two angels at the top of *The Tree of Life* from *The Kabbalah*. Enoch was aided by Arch Angel Michael to transform his human body into a body of light or Merkabah.

Attaining this, God invited Enoch to ascend to Heaven and reside at the side of God and became known as the Arch Angel Metatron. Arch Angel Michael is also associated with the Sun—as the angel of protection for humans. By invoking and following in the steps of these most exalted of angels you can be nothing less than being aided to manifest the body immortal.

This chapter also covered the two Sanskrit mantras devoted to the Sun, light (Agna) and fire (Yagna), *The Gayatri Mantra* and *The Mahamrityonjaya Mantra* and the ability to alter brainwaves into an alpha-theta level, and move our bodies more fully into the modes of light and fire. Concurrent with this, we potentiate telomerase enzyme in our bodies and HGH and by now, we should understand just how important that is.

Related to these two Sanskrit Mantras, Hey Resh Chet, which means connected to the light and the 59th Name of God from Exodus was depicted, as were other ways to bring more light and fire into our bodies, such as through sun bathing and sun gazing. Remember, most sunscreens prevent Vitamin D from being absorbed into the human body and most likely the rays of the sun as well. Also addressed was the need to concentrate on breathing the *Intelligent Cosmic Vibration* into the body through the Kriya Kundalini Pranayam(a) breath and using the Sanskrit mantras to attract the light and fire into the body, likewise. "Hey Resh Chet" is associated with the angel, Harahel.

The other angel who was suggested be invoked in our lives as well, was Achaiah, the Angel of Patience, conjunct with the seventh Name of God from Exodus, "Aleph Kaf Aleph," which invokes a state of perfection into our lives. Another personage of great repute, Elisha, although not considered an angel, ascended into the Heavens in a ball of light. It is this morphic resonance field we attempt to cultivate... to follow in the footsteps of those who have gone before us. In the end, however, we will never follow in the footsteps of any master until our "vessel" is ready to sail. Hence, the need for what we have covered so far in a far so manner. Invoking the angels can be accomplished through repeatedly saying their names in meditation, as per "Michael, reveal thyself."

Chapter Six: **We** found a full chapter in a purview of the real possibility of living without food, as per Peter Arthur Straubinger's documentary, *In the Beginning There Was Light*. We also considered the idea that a mechanistic view of calories fueling our body has never been proven and that blood sugar, glucose, glycogen—as a means of creating the body fuel of Adeno triphosphate (ADT)—can be replaced by a photosynthesis via oxidative phosphorylation, where hydrogen, oxygen and carbon create ATP, and where sunlight reacting with melanin and/or water in the human body also create ATP, in conjunction with Magnesium.

While it is believed calories are the only way to fuel a body, we uncovered the fact that almost one fourth of the human body's fuel comes from outside of the body itself, as per Dr. Webb's research that was cross validated by Durnin

178

and Dr. Riggins in his book, *The Myth of the Calorie*. We also have the function of photosynthesized ADT as a source of bodily fuel. We also have the concept of Prana/Chi/God life force, which represents electromagnetic energy and poses the question whether this makes it possible to run a body entirely on Prana/Chi/Kundalini? In the purview of the discipline of Kriya Kundalini Pranayam, this would naturally follow!

The answer to this possibility would be, "Yes, by at least two measures, since Herrera, et al., discovered there is a human photosynthesis, very similar to what occurs in trees and plants." Secondly, there is also a reaction between sunlight and the water, inside our bodies that creates a compound known as H_3O_2, called EZ-water; this creates a photosynthesized energy in our bodies, through the process of oxidative phosphorylation.

Related to this, we discovered how *The Intelligent Cosmic Vibration*—comprised of light, fire and vibration/the primal sound of creation, Om/Aum—is in fact infused into our bodies through the inhalation (in breath) and then remains in our bodies through an extended exhaling, when we perform the Kriya Kundalini Pranayam extended breathing protocol. It should be pointed out the Pranayam breath's extremely extended exhalation is what allows *The Intelligent Cosmic Vibration* to remain inside the body for a longer duration than a normal breathing cadence of equal inhalation and exhalation.

The body may be able to be fueled with Prana/Chi from the soul... the aura/etheric energy around all living bodies, and is augmented through Kriya Kundalini Pranayam and the Tai Chi Standing Meditation. This validates two methods in which the body can be supported without food, making Peter Arthur Straubinger's documentary, *In the Beginning was Light,* something we can accomplish with the corresponding ways the body can maintain itself... with only light/Prana.

We also cannot ignore that the "bulk water" from our municipal water systems is not only energetically dead but contains high levels of Deuterium that also lowers its energy potential. H_3O_2 and glaciated water, deep well water and river water are all highly energized and very low in Deuterium.

Chapter Seven: The conversation in this chapter covered the power of the pyramid, spire, steeple and dome form in attracting and magnifying light, fire, Prana, Chi, Kundalini and God life force. The benefit... is bringing the body into a state of increased light and Prana and the immortality benefits there from. After reading this chapter, we should have a new awareness of the alpha and theta brainwaves that come from meditating and how just being under a pyramid will stimulate telomerase enzyme that will keep our body from deteriorating. Proof was offered of the power of the type of energy coming into a human body with Kirilian photographs and Magnetic Field Photos. We further know the temperature closely surrounding a pyramid to be higher than measured at more distant points from the pyramid. Additionally, We were able to view pictures of people whose auras influenced by pyramid energies, which create expanded auric fields.

The chapter also included a discovery of piezoelectric minerals, including quartz, topaz and tourmaline, how they resonate with and augment the torus/pranic energies of a pyramid, and how these minerals, alone, can also aid us into the realms of deeper meditation and the brainwaves that stimulate telomerase enzyme, in the alpha and especially theta range. Again, please refer to *Pathways to God: Experiencing the Energies of the Living God in Your Everyday Life* for additional information about quartz, topaz, tourmaline and other gemstones. We also discussed how the different pyramid angles affect the human body and we discovered the 52-degree angle of the Great Pyramid in Giza, Egypt resonates with human heart; and the steeper angled pyramids, such as Khafre, in Giza, Egypt, at 53+ degree angle and the recently constructed Russian pyramids at more than 60-degree angle would resonate closer with the crown chakra, at 59-degrees the "third eye" or Pineal gland, at 58-degrees. The Russian pyramids might even be perceived as a cosmic antenna, into higher dimensions and civilizations, because of their very steep angles.

Next, we examined how to use geomagnetic leylines to achieve a deeper state of meditation and raise the energy potential of our bodies. We also covered how to create your own leyline vortex intersection.

Chapter Eight; We covered different substances such as Alcoholic beverages and Cannabis will cause the human brain to exhibit the altered state of alpha brainwaves. We further covered how Ayahuasca (DMT), LSD, Psilocybin, Ecstasy (MSMD) and Mescaline not only elicit alpha brainwaves but the higher consciousness theta brainwaves. It appears there is a lasting benefit from using these substances to more permanently shifting our consciousness into the theta realm when we are not under the influence of these substances; and again, as well as eliciting more psychic abilities and creativity and problem solving, we get the benefit of more telomerase enzyme being produced in our bodies, thus circumventing the cycle of death, or at least extending our lifespan.

Now, we also have the Ormus "White Gold Powder" or gaseous gold as a life extension agent, much of that possibly attributed to the octahedron form of gold on the atomic level. We know the Anunaki/Sumerians used this substance, which could well be attributed to the nine hundred + year's life spans found in *The Bible/The Torah*. We have come to know that elite scientists like Newton and Bacon and many ancient Arabic alchemists were searching for the secret of an eternal immortalized body.

Additionally, we covered how certain foods are a drag on the body, since they do not create enough Bovis units to keep a body in a healthy state. These debilitating foods include, meats, cooked and steamed foods and foods that create enough energy for health include raw vegetable, fresh fruits and fruit juices, wheat grass and many types of sprouts and nuts. We discovered how acidic foods like meat and alcoholic beverages do not allow enough negative ions in our bodies, which uplift us emotionally and physically; and we found that meats and beers will create nitrosamines in the human intestines, that can lead to intestinal cancer, Crohn's Disease, diverticulitis, colitis and IBS.

Chapter Nine: We viewed how negative ions will make us feel better and healthier yet our urban environments destroy negative ions through electrical technologies and microwaves. Yet we can move to or visit areas that have a natural higher concentration of negative ions like the mountains, streams, the breaking waves in an ocean and the sand there about. There are also negative ion generators for homes, businesses, and cars. There are pyramid forms that can be sat under, worn on our heads and worn as a pendant that will generate negative ions around us. Any piezoelectric mineral, including Quartz, Topaz or Tourmaline will do the same things while held in our hand or worn as a pendant. We also have ion generating infrared saunas and the Richway Bio-mat that also generate negative ions.

So from a health, longevity and immortality perspective, we know negative ions will eliminate stress and ameliorate our negative emotions. Many studies listed in Chapter Nine proved this; and here is the real reason we so vitally need these negative ions: They allow us to access the alpha and theta brainwaves, especially conjunct with states of meditation, where more telomerase enzyme will be produced inside **is nothing to lose and a lot to be gained by being bathed in negative ions and a lot to lose from not being so!**

Chapter Ten: We went deeper into how hydrogen and oxygen make it possible for us to live without food/glucose/glycogen, replacing glycogen oxidation with the process of phosphorylation involving the oxidation of water and/or melanin in reaction with sunlight and Prana/Chi breathed into a body during Kriya Kundalini Pranayam(a) and the Tai Chi "Standing Meditation. So what we get in this process of oxidative phosphorylation is an EZ-water, known as H_3O_2, which creates the body fuel ATP (Adeno triphosphate) which is then converted to ADT . So we are especially searching for water with a higher Hydrogen content to ingest and we find such in deep well water, glaciated water and in rivers. The "bulk water" from municipal water systems is devoid of Torus/vortex energies and also laden with toxic amounts of Deuterium and only has one atom of hydrogen. With outside hydrogen supplementation, Australian decathlon champion, John O'Neill, has found he can have extended periods of exercise with very little exhaustion or the build up of lactic acid in his muscles.

What we are most interested in is finding a non-caloric source of body energy... that which can be manifested without calories, glucose and glycogen and so an excess of hydrogen is the key to that. So we have Dr. Gerald Pollack's EZ-water filter that twists bulk, domestic water and infuses it will more hydrogen. We also have MJ Pangman and Melanie Evans' Dancing with Water hydrogen supplements "Active H_2," and "Prime H_2." These supplements also help with counteracting free radical damage, discussed by Dr. Patrick Flanagan.

Chapter Eleven: We considered how to get off the Wheel of Karma, which has literally been an albatross around the collective necks of humanity. We contemplated that since we are already in a state of perfection, it is ludicrous to accept we need around 2000 life times and 100,000-140,000 years of living to jump off "the wheel. Also, when we bring Sir Isaac Newton's "Third Law of Motion" we learn that for every action there is an equal and opposite reaction, so the effects of our Karma are immediately experienced and not something that haunts us over an extended period of time—or at least it does not have to necessarily be this way.

| CHAPTER THIRTEEN

NOW, ARE WE READY TO BE WEANED
FROM A HUMAN BODY
AND ASSUME OUR DIVINE GENES?
REMEMBER THE FOUNDATION OF ALL CREATION,
THE ATOM, IS 99.5% MASSLESS.

Are you ready for the body immortal?
Something that is only a lighted portal,
Loaded with photons beyond belief,
Finally a body that provides earthy relief!
Dr. Robert J. Newton, 3-7-16

WOW! THANK YOU for going on such a wide-ranging, intense journey together with me; I trust it has been both challenging and exhilarating and that you have seen many things in greater clarity. As an author, teacher, speaker, counselor, and seeker of expanded awareness, I have been nourished and energized at a scientific and spiritually esoteric level. We need to always keep in mind that everything in the cosmos is energy and most likely will never be otherwise. Our Creator is only energy and we are mini versions thereof. Think of God as a huge molecule and we as the individual atoms that comprise that molecule. If we are made in the image and likeness of God and we are atoms, we know that God is likewise, made of atoms. That is so very fortuitous for us and much more so than most people are ready to fully comprehend and/or accept. **Too many of our compatriots have been taught there is only one way to salvation, immortality, and a blissful union with our Creator... and that is to die first!**

As much as possible with words and images, I have shared how this simply is not the case, even though there are those, like certain friends I have known for decades, who feel I am possessed by evil spirits! Certain people may make such proclamations from a state of ignorance about God as the Creator and perfect creation of man and Nature. My message is delivered in light of the "Nine Geometric Forms of Creation" on an atomic level and from amazing fractal geometries liberally dispersed through Nature—manifested in fruits and vegetables, and in the trees and plants on our earthly level, and even extending into the galactic level.

Granted, it would be most helpful if we understood more about the myriad aspects of the energy of cells. It seems easier to understand our multi-miles-long strands of DNA are energy, since if it were otherwise... it would never fit within our bodies. In *Our Cells: A Molecular Approach, 2nd Ed.*, by Geoffrey M. Cooper, I found knowledge that begins to hint at the real nature of cells, even though his approach is from a molecular standpoint. Molecular or not, what I take from his book is finding **the same carbon and water in cells---just coincidentally containing hydrogen and oxygen, which just happens to manifest into a most amazing body fuel, H_2O_3.** I fervently want readers to see the similarities I do; the same kind of similarity we see in the blood, as referenced in Chapter Ten, where carbon, hydrogen and oxygen are formed into molecules inside the cells. Although cell biologists would disagree with this, I would have you embrace the possibility this is the same process and energy reaction going on in the cells—as ATP is in the blood. It definitely is a process of combustion/energy production that is transported to the cells **and not material in nature**, As Cooper well describes, there are carbohydrates, lipids, proteins and nucleic acids inside the cells as a type of food. Yet it is the CHO_3 molecule comprised of carbon, hydrogen and three atoms of oxygen and the polar opposites (negative and positive charges) in the atoms, which coalesces the molecule and the electricity or Prana from the polar opposites.

Could it be at this point these "foods" are ignited into corresponding types of energy, which are esoterically known as Prana and Chi and scientifically known as electromagnetic energy?

The questions still remain: "Can this happen in a state of perpetuity?" and "Can the carbohydrates, lipids, proteins and nucleic acids be summoned into the body without food?" So far, I have not found if and/or how this is done! Yet we do have H_3O_2 providing the elements to create the body fuel of Adeno triophosphate (ATP)! I then contend, "If things cannot be done one way—they can be manifested in another fashion—as the Creator is a most ingenious and creative presence, and inextricably, so are we... everyone of us!"

This diagram reveals the hydrogen-carbon-oxygen molecule in our body cells where Adeno triphosphate (ADT) is created and released as energy. The real question is, "Do these cells have to wear out and/or can they be replicated indefinitely by the telomere in the chromosomes of the DNA?"

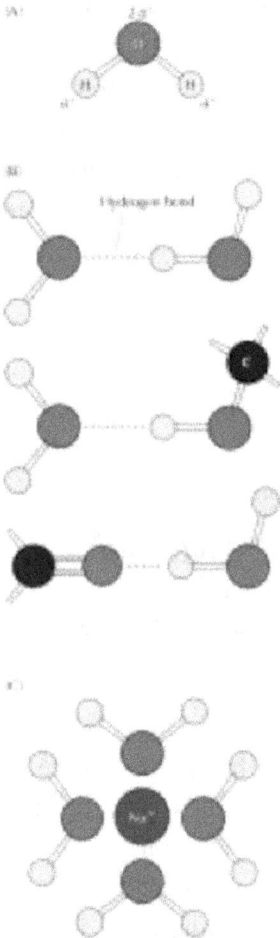

FIG #27

In the May, 2012 MIT Technology Review, there was an article, *Biophoton Communication: Can Cells Really Talk with Light,* which reveals evidence of cell communication via bio-photons. This is significant in two ways. First it reveals a light factor (the Biophoton(s)), Agna, Kundalini, Prana, Chi in the cells via photons therein, by the cells. Secondly, **cells comprised of light and a body of light/energy really should not need food, nor the components thereof, to exist in a vibrant, immortalized existence.** I am concluding this from the depth of science as exists and from *The Bhagavad Gita* and Babaji Nagaraj's, *The Death of Death*. Since Babaji Nagaraj is the last person I know of who entered the state of Soruba Samadhi/immortality, other than Mataji and Nogababa. What sources and what people might actually know more about this subject? **And... since the three people listed above are in immortalized bodies, their body cells probably have not expired either or so it should seem.**

Light, Agna and Fire... Yagna, could easily be an alternative fuel instead of carbohydrates, lipids, proteins and nucleic acids, and could be vastly superior as a perpetual source of fuel to power a body since such energy exists in boundless quantities, on Earth and elsewhere!

I am not certain we can get to an immortalized body through a cellular approach, **other than the bio photonic cell approach, just mentioned, because the photonic properties come from non deteriorating atoms**; but I know there are some amazing studies (and progress) taking place in the process of oxidative phosphorylation creating H_3O_2 that produces ATP without calories, glucose or glycogen, and sun and light appear to be what makes this possible. Adding the light and fire breathed into the body via Kriya Kundalini Pranayam and protocols discussed in the beginning of the book, this process certainly could be a real factor to create the oxidative phosphorylation like trees and plants.

I exist in a state of Samadhi (the cessation of breathing and heart beats) or quasi Samadhi for hours' duration during the day, quantified with a pulse oximeter. When I am running or paddling during surfing, the suspension is more difficult to achieve. Will that change in the future?

In the end, we really do not need a cellular approach to create sufficient energy to nourish the body. We already discovered that 23% of the energy that supports our human bodies comes from outside of the body itself, as per the research of Dr. Webb, Durnin, et al, and Dr. Riggins in *The Myth of the Calorie,* which is electromagnetic/electrical energy. What Dr. Riggins book tells us is that "calorie theory" is just that... a theory. It has never been proven as an actual photosynthesized energy from the reaction of the sun — with either melanin and/or water in the body. As much as I wanted to find a cellular way where carbohydrates, protein, lipids and nucleic acids could be transported into the cells without food, I have found no validation thereof, although oxidative phosphorylation does, and leads to the production of, ATP and Redox cells that are regenerated or replicated in the body, as well.

Right now, in this here and now, we can get off The Wheel of Karma and attain a state of illumination and a commensurate immortality.

I previously shared how this shift can be accomplished; however, one of the last known persons to have attained this state of immortality, Babaji Nagaraj, says it possibly better, with more cogency and authority than I can muster. In *The Death of Death* Satguru Babaji writes, "Be good, do good, be humble, be pure, be compassionate, you will attain illumination." **Anyone and everyone can do this!** It simply takes the discipline you attain in the Kriya Dhyana

Meditation, Eka Nilai—the one point—and the focus derived there from. Then all else that is needed to start this journey is an **intense desire that leads to a regular disciplined practice of Kriya Dhyana and Kriya Kundalini Pranayam.** The following, then, is the regimen I share with you, in conjunction with what I have taught a limited number of students:

#1: Become initiated into Kriya Kundalini Yoga, much sooner than later. Make this a priority in your life schedule. You can do that with me by connecting on my website: www.drrobertnewton.com/.

Regular practice provides you with the discipline of the six Kriya Dhyana Meditations that will **calm and focus your mind.** You will learn the six Pranayam(a) breathing protocols that I call a meditation, for lack of a better word, that will infuse your body with The Intelligent Cosmic Vibration discussed on numerous occasions in the book, and its components—including Yagna (fire) and Agna (light), which equate to Prana/Chi/God Life Force and Aum/Om— The Primal Sound of Creation.

Kriya Kundalini Yoga practices will create and **multiply alpha and theta brainwaves, creating a direct pathway to our Creator/God** (yog/yug means union... a union with God) and multiplying alpha and theta brainwaves. It will also stimulate more telomerase enzyme that seems to be the keep the cells of the body, properly regenerated. How often and how long these things need to be practiced will be shared in your Kriya Kundalini Yoga initiation. Some people will experience ringing in the ears after doing assiduous amounts of Pranayam(a). The antidote for this is practicing less Pranayam and yet doing so works against our purpose here. For myself, I have lived with a continuous ringing of the ears for ten year and there are benefits from this, including cancelling negative brain programming. For me, this is a biofeedback that I am getting close to immortalizing my body.

Remember a relaxed body is a body much more infused with Chi and Prana because the body muscles and joints do not have tension therein. Furthermore, a relaxed body will create the meditative states of alpha and theta brainwaves, where the facilitation of telomerase enzyme occurs and quite possibly HGH, as well. The Tai Chi Standing Meditation and Kriya Kundalini Yoga and its components of Asana, Kriya Dhyana/Dharana and Kriya Kundalini Pranayam further relaxation and the more beneficial brainwaves of alpha, theta and even upper delta and the connection to the Divine realms.

These are details we can use to keep more Prana/Chi in our bodies by keeping our mouths closed during meditation and Pranayam(a). This applies to our daily routine, as well and we also need to concentrate on keeping the anus as tight as possible, as much Prana/Chi can leak there from. People who talk a lot, are wasting significant Prana, as well. Also, people who live in tropical areas of high temperature, lack Agna (fire) and are more prone to a death urge; hence, people in these areas need to perform more Pranayam(a) to compensate for this! This information was gleaned my reading *Physical Immortality* by Leonard Orr.

The Immortality Prophecy

When your body becomes more infused with Prana and when the brainwaves become entrained in alpha and especially theta, you will be able to enter Samadhi, after performing 48 continuous repetitions of Kriya Kundalini Pranayam(a) after four to six months of a twice-daily practice of Pranayam at a 25-40 second breathing cycle; this is an extended breathing regimen with the 48 continuous repetitions. Your breathing will either stop or slow down vastly and your heart will stop beating or very slowly. **This is why you need a seasoned teacher to teach you this and be with you, if possible, when you go into Samadhi and/or a Kundalini energy infusion.** The first experience in Samadhi might last only fifteen or twenty minutes or it might last an hour or more. You can also have a Kundalini Awakening when practicing Samadhi; things can get really intense and requires you really use a teacher/guide to move through the incredible intensity of all the Kundalini energy and deep dimensional shifts you may experience.

Eventually, your experiences in Samadhi will get longer and can extend into several hours at a time. You might experience Samadhi when involved in your daily routine. The more Kriya Kundalini Pranayam you perform, the more benefits therefrom ye shall reap. Kriya Kundalini Yoga and especially, Pranayam, is more than enough to enter a state of bodily immortality. The Satguru/Avatars—who have come before us, and have achieved such—make following in their footsteps much easier.

As per Sri Swami Sivananda... if you complete the 320 repetitions of Pranayam(a) he recommends, you could be blasting down the door of Samadhi and not so long thereafter, Soruba Samadhi. I have calculated this will take four to six hours to complete. The most Pranayam(a) I have done in one day is four hours, and even so—not very regularly. Another technique I teach, which seems unique relative to the practice of Pranayam is combining a silent recitation of *The Gayatri Mantra* and the *Maha Mrityunjaya Mantra* in conjunction with my sessions of Pranayam. Certainly to combine these, and the resultant invocation of The Intelligent Cosmic Vibration of Aum/Om and Yagna (fire) and Agna (light)... will speed up your pursuit of immortality. This would lessen the need for 320 repetitions of Pranayam(a).

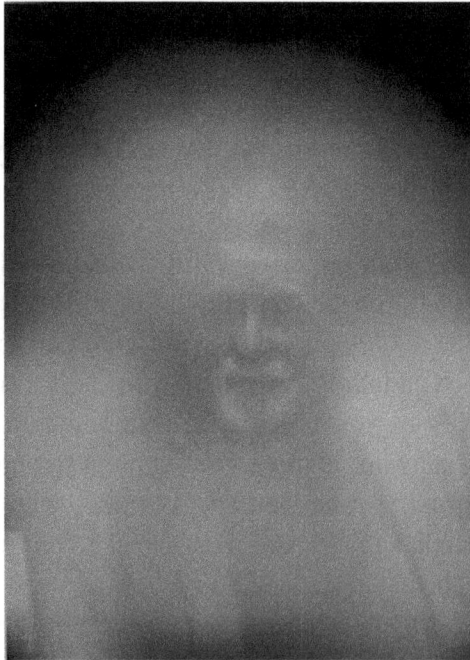

FIG #28

The above is a picture of what Kriya Kundalini Pranayam(a) can do to your aura; the image that follows reflects the changes in my aura after thirty minutes of continuous repetitions,—forty eight in number—of Kriya Kundalini Pranayam(a). At the top of the aura are the spiritual colors of purple, indigo and blue; beneath that a large field of magenta indicates strong mental powers and below the happiness seen in yellow and the healing of green. If you would like to have a full color index of all images, you can make the request from my website, as noted in the reference section at the end of the book.

FIG #29

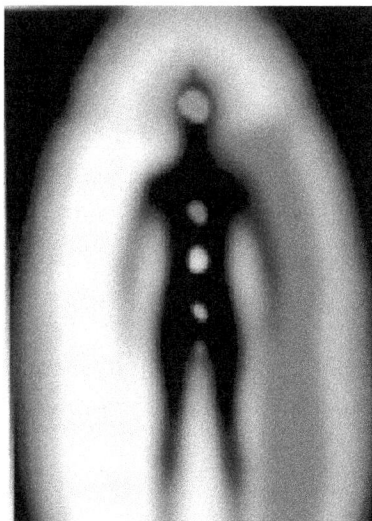

This vies represents a chakra scan shortly after performing repetitions of Kriya Kundalini Pranayam(a):

Even though not in color, in the print version in this chakra scan completed after doing Kriya Kundalini Pranayam(a), notice that all chakras are vibrant and there is an intense accumulation of energy in the Crown (top of head) Chakra. Also note the strong band of Prana on the right side denoted by red (in the color image) and the happiness denoted by a long band that is much lighter, and which would be seen in yellow on the right side of a color image. I will stand by these pictures as the proof of the power of Pranayam(a). The Kindle version of this book and versions of my other publications offer full color images that better depict what I seek to convey.

 # 2: Exercise and stretching are crucial to keep the body flexible, properly aligned and energized. I may have been remiss in not mentioning the importance of Yoga Asanas (stretching) and general stretching and exercise throughout the book because I know as a fact that the health of an unexercised and unstretched body begins to decline after the age of forty and **exercise has been demonstrated to create the conditions to produce. Telomerase enzyme**. This deterioration is attributed to the body no longer being able to regenerate cells like it did when we were younger. The telomerase enzyme discussed in several places herein will certainly help this problem, protecting the telomeres and their ability to replicate new cells. However, there is another factor to this that is far too frequently ignored, which is that the **Prana/Chi in the body need to be moved throughout the body.** Yoga Asanas, stretching, and exercise serve to perpetuate the movement of energy throughout the body.

It has been revealed from research of exercise physiology that microbursts of exercise are much better than a continuous aerobic workout for thirty to forty five minutes. This could involve a one to several minute(s) duration of intense running, biking, jumping jacks, etc. at full bore, followed by a slow and easy performance of these types of exercise followed by another several minutes microburst of exercise and then ten minutes of slow exercise and repeating this for three to five total cycles, performed three to five times per week.

Please do not ignore this! I know I have said this before but it is important; I know of several Yogi's, with highly developed psychic and spiritual powers, whose bodies degenerated rather quickly after the cessation of Yoga Asanas, stretching and exercising and soon thereafter they died. I recommend the "Aging Backwards" stretching program, by Maria Edmond-White, in place of Yoga Asanas, if you so desire, to counteract muscle, joint and spinal degeneration and to keep enervated. Whether an immortalized body of light functions well without stretching and exercise I have not ascertained at this point in time. Certainly Pranayam and Tai Chi and Qui Gong move a lot of energy throughout the body but is that enough?

 # 3: Learn, become initiated into, and start reciting *The Gayatri Mantra, The Mahamrityunjay Mantra, and The Aum/Om Mantra.* These three mantras are the most powerful Sanskrit mantras and I already shared the cymatic/vibrational power of them in Chapter Three. There are also several Babaji Nagaraj Sanskrit Mantras that will give you an immediate energy connection and guidance from Babaji, who has already gone down this pathway we are we are on and his "inner guidance" has invaluable for me, including the sharing of things related to Kriya Kundalini Yoga, extant in no text I have found on Earth. Additionally, for those of you who have qualms about religions, which I have myself, Yoga is not a religion yet rather the study, practice and union (Yog), with the Creator/God. Practice the designated mantras at least 108 continuous repetitions at least once per day. This would be the minimum; the more you do the more you are going to infuse your body with "The Intelligent Cosmic Vibration" and the light and cymatic power therein.

Ignore this if you like having a material body and its many maladies (joke)! **The Sanskrit mantras are practiced sub-vocally**, which means they are repeated in your head. It is taught this will hold and infuse the body more fully with the mantra. Again, I can initiate you into this if you connect with me on my website as well as Yogi Govindan, whose information is also listed in the Resource section. Also, I have a mantra MP3 I recorded of the Om/Aum, Gayatri and Maha Mrityunjaya Sanskrit mantra available on my website. I encourage you to consider using the Solfeggio frequency of the 528 Hz. and the diatonic frequency of 440 Hz. as ways to activate a higher light factor within the human body. There are recordings concentrating on these and the whole range of Solfeggio Frequencies.

 # 4: Get a copy of "The 72 Names of God" from Exodus 14: 19-21 from the Kabbalah Center and purchase their book, by Rabbi Yehuda Berg, *The 72 Names of God: Technology for the Soul*. Study these names at least daily, learn them in Hebrew and use the unique protocol I shared in Chapter Four of *A Map to Healing and Your Essential Divinity Through Theta Consciousness* and use the names therein to heal and "anoint" and reprogram your body with light. This is a light infusion and healing protocol, starting out with "Chet Resh Hey" and is something revealed to me after I had studied and recited the names for about two years.

Studying these names is going to help alter your consciousness into alpha and theta brainwaves. Memorize these names and learn how to pronounce then in Hebrew, because there is a cymatic or vibrational therapeutic benefit from doing so that brings the human body more closely into its true form of light (refer back to the cymatic pictures of the atomic magic that takes place in the language of Hebrew— Fig. 11.

 # 5: Consider eating much less food and make sure the food you do eat is alkalized in nature (raw vegetables, fruits, beans and certain grains like Quinoa, Buckwheat, Millet, Bulgur Wheat, Brown Rice and shun meats, alcoholic beverages and sugary desserts. Concentrate on eating a large variety of nuts, sprouts and drinks with algae, wheatgrass and barley grass. Keep your body in a state of 7.2 Ph., by concentrating on alkalized foods... sprouts, sprouted grain bread, algae, wheatgrass, barley grass, Spirulina and Chlorella Algae.

After your initial transition, consider fasting for a few days at a time, ingesting only liquids—especially water and fresh fruit juices. You will most likely feel much better after your fasts and this will prepare the way to transitioning to a Breathairian diet, ingesting only liquids. You could also change over to a diet of fresh fruits. Another suggestion... ingest large amounts of Tulsi Tea, as Tulsi, *Occinum Sanctum* will create a deep relaxation in the human body, which will create alpha and theta brainwaves, and more telomerase enzyme and infuse the body with a higher factor of Prana/Chi/light. Do not do any of this if you have diagnosed medical problems or strong *doubts* about your ability to do so or do this at your own risk! However, this is your decision and responsibility to decide. In *Breaking the Death Habit,* Leonard Orr discuses how fasting will make food taste better.

Reprogram your brain/mind, eliminating those mind programs that tell you it is impossible to live without food and replace these with the 43rd Name of God, "Vav Vav Lamed," which relates to making the impossible possible. The Breathairian "diet" should be done in conjunction with Kriya Kundalini Pranayam, and/or sun gazing and sun bathing and the Tai Chi "Standing Meditation" so as help initialize the process of body photosynthesis, which is oxidative phosphorylation. Breathairianism is an essential step to achieve an immortalized body of light… a Merkabah!

Once again, do not attempt the breathairian approach to nitrifying the human body if you have diagnosed medical conditions and/or strong doubts whether this can be done. You must decide, at your own risk, what will be your course of action! Remember, in light of all of this, that **every study on a calorie restricted diet on rats and humans, always reveals extended life spans, there from.** Overeating definitely shortens life span and increases disease and sickness within a body! *Caveat emptor!*

 # 6: I would also recommend **Studying the Builders of the Adytum** (BOTA) lessons; they will infuse you with the Alchemical knowledge of Dr. Paul Foster Case, through the Hermetic Order of the Golden Dawn and the Masonic Blue Lodge systems. Dr. Case also was a practitioner of Kriya

Kundalini Yoga so there is a natural connection here. The BOTA lessons focus on teaching you esoteric psychology (similar to Dr. Carl Jung), numerology, occult Tarot, Hermetic Kabbalah (including "The 72 Names of God" from "Exodus" in *The Torah),* and Astrology... in an integrated and more meaningful manner, than is now dispensed on planet Earth. Although Dr. Case was an elevated soul of great knowledge and a world-class pianist, he is an Avatar, even though he never claimed or aspired to this venerated status.

 # 7: Decide which path to sexuality you are going to follow: the Taoist and Tantric approach or the chastity, Brahmacharya protocols—and refrain from sexuality. Stick with the Brahmacharya unless you come to the realization, as have I, it is impossible to become sexually depleted through a union with the female or male forms. The type of sexuality I am discussing is based on Taoist and Tantric concepts... not group sex, bondage or other perversions of sacred sexuality; nor is it based on lust.

> *When a spiritually based orgasm is*
> *experienced, we are essentially in a union with*
> *our Creator through the Prana and Chi God*
> *shares with us.*

The Tantric and Taoist approaches to sexuality, which are previously discussed, will lead you to the spiritually focused orgasm It is also described multiple times in my third book, *The Hidden Codes of God.*

 # 8: Focus on bringing more Hydrogen into the human body. The reasons for this are well documented in Chapters

Six and Ten and even this chapter. We can do this as simply as sun bathing and sun gazing. We can do this during Kriya Kundalini Pranayam(a) extended breathing meditation. We can do so through infusing our water with Hydrogen via Dr. Gerald Pollack's EZ-water filter or with the "Dancing with Waters" Hydrogen supplements such as "Active H_2" and "Prime H_2" and the Hydrogen Water filter pitcher. There is also the John Ellis Water Machine which make you water infused with H_2O_2 (Hydrogen Peroxide). Why would we do these things? Because we want a condition of H_3O_2 or H_2O_2 existing within our bodies so as to counteract free radical damage, as well as to create the condition of oxidative phosphorylation, whereby we circumvent creating ATP with glucose and glycogen and replace that process using Oxygen to oxidize Hydrogen into ATP, that fuels our bodies.

 # 9: Do everything possible to keep your body in the brainwave states, in alpha and theta, which allow a continual production of telomerase enzyme. So the benefit of sexual union has been shown to promote this as has all types of meditation, but especially Kriya Kundalini Pranayam(a). We have covered how dancing and exercise help promote these higher brainwaves, as does music, singing and Sanskrit mantras, especially Om/Aum, Gayatri and Maha Mrityunjaya. Remember, the mantras need to be recited 108 times consecutively for the most effect and benefit. We get this also from negative ionic sources such as pyramids, the piezo electric minerals of Quartz, Topaz and Tourmaline. We also get negative ions at the beach, other sources of moving water, and in the mountains.

#10: Spend some time everyday under a pyramid, and use piezo electric minerals. The following magnetic field photograph taken of me under a pyramid will give proof of the reasons why. Not only is a human body going to be more infused with Prana/Chi/God life force, negative ions and alpha and theta brainwaves and hence more telomerase enzyme. This is a really effective type of immortality multi tasking with three major benefits. Add in the use of Quartz, Topaz and Tourmaline with being under a pyramid, either holding one of these piezo electric minerals in your left hand or as a pendant around your neck and you magnify the three benefits increased Prana, negative ions and the shift into alpha and theta brainwaves. Would doing this in a seven or twelve leyline intersection or vortex further intensify these benefits? Yes. **Never limit your creativity!**

There is a certain amount of vulnerability in sharing the following image of me... under a holographic eight inch gold plated pyramid. The picture depicts intense life force energies coming into his body, denoted in red in the color rendering, combined below with the happiness of yellow and the healing colors of green.

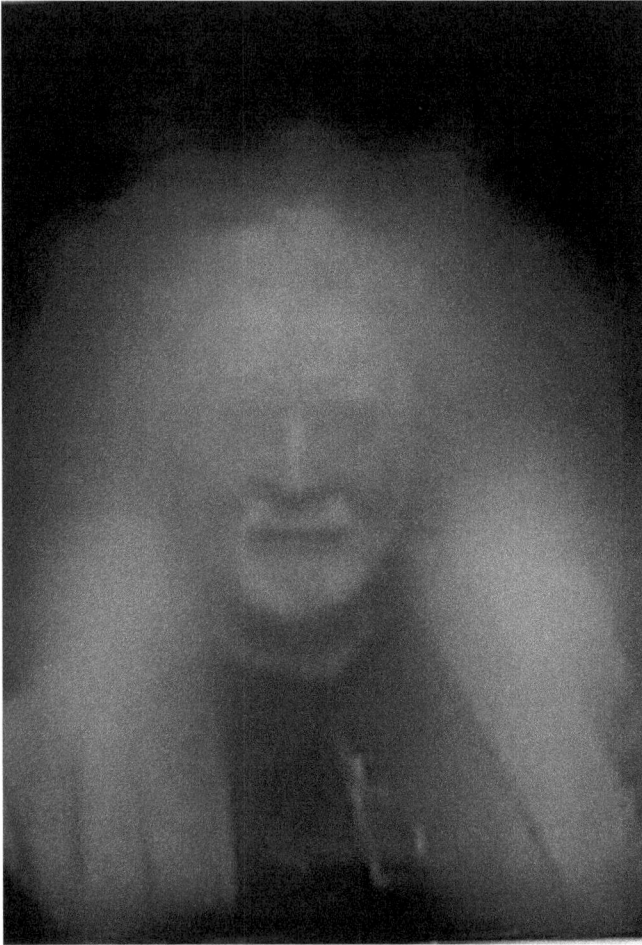

FIG #30

#11: Utilize the angel connections shared herein as connections to immortality. This includes Enoch/Archangel Metatron, associated with light and Archangel Michael, associated with the Sun, which is equates to light and fire. Both of these angels are at the top of Kabbalistic "Tree of

Life," on the left and right side of God/Yahweh. The power of these of these two angels is unparalleled in the Kabala and meditating upon their names invokes their presence and the higher factors of light that are associated with them. Also, there is great power in the "Tree of Life" angel, Ankaiah, who is associated with the seventh and most powerful names of "The 72 Names of God", "Aleph Kaf Aleph"…restoring things to their perfect state. Invoking Ankaiah's name, we invoke the perfection, which we always were and will always be. When we invoke the angel, Harahel, we are invoking the 59th Name of God, "Hey Resh Chet" and connecting ourselves to the light.

#12: Consider using Ormus and other hallucinogenic/ psychotropic substances as aids to achieving altered and higher consciousness and the substances and supplements that help to stimulate telomerase enzyme. The Ormus and supplements would be recommended without qualification. The Hallucinogenic substances would be recommended for limited use, to open the brain and consciousness up to the altered brainwaves of alpha-theta and the production of more telomerase enzyme. The Pranayam(a) breathing meditation has innumerable benefits the hallucinogenic substances can prepare us to perform such… a bridge thereto, in a manner of speaking. It is definitely within the purview of Kriya Kundalini Pranayam and the Tai Chi "Standing Meditation" to naturally take us into the highest levels consciousness, which is initiated by the use of Cannabis, Ayahuasca Psilocybin, Mescaline, Peyote, Ecstasy and LSD. The reason for doing this is to be able to access the higher dimensions at will, sans substances. We need our consciousness to be in the alpha-theta range as much as possible. The more we are anchored in alpha-theta, the more we become enlightened (en-light-ened or shrouded in light), with the emphasis being on light—and the benefits a body derives there from—namely, moving us into a Merkabah (body of light).

#13: Use the words with the Gematria equivalents to immortality and such as 101, 110, 1 and 0 with similarities to light and love that are contained in Chapter Four. Remember to stay happy as per the first and 49th name of God, Vav Hey Vav. This is much easier to do when you:

Recite this particular name;
Laugh and are being goofy;
Sing and whistle; and when you
Dance.

Happiness begets more happiness...
it is like an infectious virus. When you are
happy you are in the alpha and theta
brainwaves, which keep us healthier and
producing lots of telomerase enzyme and HGH.

You will also pull yourself into the higher dimensions of functioning—where everything is easier to accomplish, because you are relaxed and happy! You can **never laugh too much!** Enough said?

#14: Although this is somewhat redundant, this point cannot be over emphasized. **Meditate and perform Pranayam(a) as much as possible. Realize it is very possible to meditate**

as you work, exercise, sing and dance. Yes, for real! The Shamatha Project, led by Fahri Saatcioglu at the University of Oslo, determined intensive meditators had thirty percent longer telomere strands in their DNA. This same study found Yoga Asanas and deep Yogic breathing, via Sudarshan Kriya Yoga and meditation, elicit a relaxation response that has a long term effect on "gene expression" and when the telomere strands were lengthened a person's immune system was strengthened.

In a study by Taakroo, Bhavanani, Pal, Udupa and Krishnamurthy at the Pondcherry Police Training School,[13] the police trainees practiced Asana and Pranayam and there were significant increases in alpha and theta brainwaves and even some delta waves. Also, it was shown the trainees could process data quicker, which certainly proves the importance of meditation... and then some!

Just remember, as Patanjali's *The Yoga Sutras,* reveal, each breath of the Pranayam(a) breath is taken into a body, our lives are lengthened. As the Chinese breathing canons and in the book, *The Primordial Breath: An Ancient Chinese Way of Prolonging Life Through Breath Control,* translated by Jane Huang, reveals, life can definitely be extended through breath control. Giant Sea Turtles and Whales have life spans into the three and four hundred year range and that is because they only take one breath every three to four minutes, and what this does is infuse a body with Oxygen, Hydrogen and the Prana (electromagnetic energy/electricity) that pulls these

---

[13] http://www.ncbi.nlm.nih.gov/pubmed/23930027

into the lungs. At worst, this would put the whales and sea turtles in a quasi state of Samadhi, if not Samadhi itself.

If you need a bit of "recall" simply read again what we covered about oxidative phosphorylation where hydrogen and oxygen create ATP that fuels our bodies without food/calories/glucose/glycogen.

Also, consider the short life spans of dogs that pant and breathe short all the time. There is very little infusion of Prana/light/Hydrogen/Oxygen into the body of a dog. So these extremes prove the point of the connection between extended breathing and extended life spans.

So here is another study that reveals the power of the Pranayam(a) meditation. Drs. Leela, Mallikarjun, Prafulla and Swapnali, as reported in *The International Research Journal of Pharmacy and Plant Science* in "The Effect of Pranayama and Yoga on Apolipoproteins, Lipid profile and Atherogenic Index in Healthy Subjects,"[14] that found vastly lower levels of harmful cholesterol in the study subjects. There are other tests done showing the MTT Cell Analysis of the cells of people practicing Kundalini Yoga and Pranayam, a component thereof, was much higher than the test subjects not practicing Pranayam. A 967% mitochondrial cell energy increase regarding this was validated in Dr. Jeffrey Dusek's study at the Harvard Medical School in July 2008.

---

[14] http://soushrutam.com/010203.pdf

#15: You might want to learn about the **Indian regenerative medicine, known as Kaya Kalpa**. When I often queried Yogi Govindan Satchidanada about this, he would consistently reply there was no known connection to this ancient knowledge and it is not even contained in Satguru, Babaji Nagaraj's, *The Death of Death*. There is some information about this to glean from the Internet, yet I am not highly confident about the veracity thereof. What I have shared with you is equivalent to Kaya Kalpa, if not more so.

#16: Laugh and be happy, and let it flow!

So what I have shared with you, herein, goes back to a fifty-year search. The last five years of this research have been exciting beyond anything I thought I might find fifty years ago. Here's to our immortality! This immortality of wise persons/souls would allow us to fulfill the Mayan, Hopi and Krishna prophesies of a "Golden Age." For the Mayans and Hopis, this was predicted as a thousand year time span, whereas Krishna predicted a period of ten thousand years. I set visions for how we could create a Golden Age in *Beyond the Mists of Time: When Trees Ruled the Earth* and the end of *Planet of the Stupids: Bringing the Light of God Back to Planet Earth and a Paradise Found* Experienced wise souls are needed to make this transition into a mini- Kaliyuga. This wise soul designation is rarely found in young souls and newly incarnated people.

Reincarnating over and over, after acquiring life experience and the wisdom attached thereto, is simply a waste of time and incarnations and stunts Earth's growth and ability to transform itself into a Paradise Found. So **immortality for us is not only achievable but necessary, as well!**

Living *la vida immortalis* (the life immortal),

Namaste (be blessed in the light)

Hey Resh Chet (connected to the light),

Dr. Robert J. Newton,
Pranayama Ananda

The Immortality Prophecy

REMEMBRANCE FROM LONG AGO

Coming into a realization at the age of five,
That the theology of Earth was much about jive,
Being isolated from my fellow man by my strange beliefs,
Would there ever be a time of acceptance, not just grief!
Under a dark cloud and ready to end my life,
Out of nowhere came an angel to end my strife,
A cup of cold water was offered to quench my thirst,
And knowledge was offered to remove my curse.
This changed the whole tone of my painful life,
I began to see the possibilities for immortality were rife,
Searching every nook and corner with a laser focus,
I finally realized bodily immortality was not hocus-
pocus.
Going back to the light surrounding during my
conception,
I realized that inevitable death was a real deception,
I could see the light from the soul of my incarnation,
Augmenting that light immortal into my jubilation!
Dr. Robert J. Newton, 5-20-16

As a note... that angel was Reba Hammond Lawler. I
will never forget her!

213

ADDENDUM:

This pictorial representation of dissertation is from doctoral candidate, Danny Caputi, and merits consideration. [15]

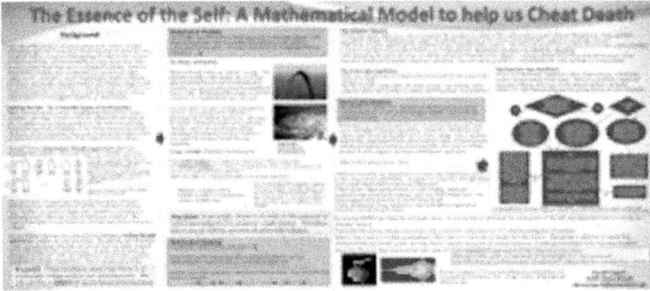

FIG #31

https://deltaaware.files.wordpress.com/2014/04/slide11.png

Right to copy given by Danny Caputi.

---

[15] https://deltaaware.files.wordpress.com/2014/04/slide11.png

ABOUT THE AUTHOR

Dr. Robert J. Newton has lived his life much in the manner he writes... with a quest to surround himself with the highest level knowledge in the myriad areas that ensure we live rich, full lives. His education has been extensive, ranging from Speech and English at Cal State Fullerton, to a Juris Doctorate from American College of Law, and many certifications in alternative healing. He formalized his career in Naturopathic Medicine as a graduate of Clayton School of Natural Healing.

Newton has lived to serve others; operating an award-winning landscape and design company for many years, as a Christian Science healer for two decades, and more recently as an author, speaker and life and relationship coach. Yoga, Metaphysics, Spiritual Sciences, Natural Healing, World Religions, Ancient Hermetic teachings... this philosopher and champion for the world has tapped into the roots of spirituality, sexuality, life and love—all with the purpose to enlighten those with a common desire to utilize multiple methods and strategies to approach life more effectively, creatively, radiantly and with great abundance.

Today, Dr. Newton lives his life looking forward... honoring the love and the beliefs he shared with his wife, and writing more novels to plant a "What if" seed in the minds of his readers.

Dr. Newton continues to provide a series of classes and book signings around North and South America, teaching and initiating people into the very things that lead to immortality. A rough outline of this is at www.drrobertnewton.com.

Please feel free to contact Dr. Newton at theta4ia@yahoo.com or at RJNewton@RobertJNewtonAuthor.com for more specifics for these events. You can also stay connected with him on the following social media platforms:

AMAZON AUTHOR CENTRAL:

http://www.amazon.com/Dr.-Robert-J.-Newton/e/B00LR6A402

WEBSITE(s): http://www.drrobertnewton.com/

http://www.robertjnewtonauthor.com/

TWITTER: https://twitter.com/drrobertjnewton

GOODREADS: https://www.goodreads.com/author/show/6076382.Robert_J_Newton

FACEBOOK:

https://www.facebook.com/robert.newton3

The Immortality Prophecy

https://www.facebook.com/pages/Dr-Robert-J-Newton-AuthorRadio-Show-Host-Motivational-Speaker/1597130127224474

BLOG: *http://www.artistfirst.com/newton.htm*

RADIO SHOW: http://www.artistfirst.com/newton.htm

The Dr. Robert J. Newton Radio Show is a lively discussion of scientific and spiritual subjects, including zero point energy, Zeitgeist (the sharing and sustaining of Earth's resources among all people, not just a few rich oligarchs), cutting edge healing modalities, mind reprogramming, developing psychic abilities and altered states of consciousness and reality.

Dr. Newton also does motivational speaking, corporate operating strategies, life success and relationship counseling. Check www.greatmotivationaltalks.com

OTHER BOOKS BY THE AUTHOR

A prolific writer, Dr. Newton brings a wide array of reading to readers who enjoy having their minds challenged in the midst of a good read. Available in various formats: Amazon paperback, Kindle, Barnes and Noble and Ivy's bookstore.

If you didn't take advantage of the invitation at the beginning of the book to become a part of my VIP Reader community, and get a little taste for some of the other writing that, as non-fiction, addresses many of the same issues discussed throughout this book, but in a little less technical manner, I am repeating that invitation here. As I indicated earlier, I am passionate—ever so passionate about the messages I am intended to deliver—and realize there are readers of every vent out there waiting for me to speak (write) in a tone that both challenges their thinking and inspires the possibilities. Join me today…

http://www.robertjnewtonauthor.com/vip-readers/

or head right over to my books page and access them at: http://bit.ly/RNewtonAuthor

218

Planet of the Stupids: Bringing Back the Light of God to Planet Earth-With a Paradise Found (March 2016)

In Search of the Body Immortal: Let the Journey Begin (October 2015)

Beyond the Mists of Time: When Trees Ruled the Earth And The State of Balance and Euphoria That Ensued There From (March 2015)

The Hidden Codes of God: A Journey to the Unknown Secrets and Dimensions of the Divine and the Energy of Love (March 2015)

Pathways to God: Experiencing the Energies of the Living God in Your Everyday Life (April, 2012)

A Map to Healing and Your Essential Divinity Through Theta Consciousness: Physics of the Immortal "Light Body" and the Creator's Template of Perfection and Abundance for His People! (March 2012)

REQUEST FOR REVIEWS

If you enjoyed reading *The Immortality Prophecy*, I would appreciate it if you would help others enjoy the book, too.

LEND IT. This book is lending enabled, so please feel free to share with a friend.

Robert J. Newton

RECOMMEND IT. Please help other readers find the book by recommending it to readers' groups, discussion boards, Goodreads, etc.

REVIEW IT. Please tell others why you liked this book by reviewing it on the site where you purchased it, on your favorite book site, or your own blog.

EMAIL ME. I'd love to hear from you. theta4ia@yahoo.com
RJNewton@RobertJNewtonAuthor.com

BIBLIOGRAPHY

[1] kadenchiropractic.com/clients/2348/documents/**Foun tain__**of_**Youth_**Handout.pdf

[2] med.stanford.edu/scopeblog/sdarticle.pd

[3] http://sanfrancisco.cbslocal.com/2014/10/18/ucsf-study-links-soda-to-premature-aging-disease-early-death/

[4] http://www.allinahealth.org/Penny-George-Institute-for-Health-and-Healing/Research/

[5] https://www.infona.pl/resource/bwmeta1.element.els evier-52b75e64-c460-3142-ac56-53bcc7deeed4

[6] http://www.fasebj.org/content/12/6/395.short

[7] http://www.ncbi.nlm.nih.gov/pmc/articles/PMC3629 142/

[8]http://www.epistemonikos.org/documents/c8ae05897 415e0a22df1271e8b45c5dfb832ac2c/

[9] http://thedea.org/docs/2005_Freedman_22686_1.pdf

[10] http://www.ncbi.nlm.nih.gov/pmc/articles/PMC219 5229/pdf/879.pdf

[11] http://www.comtech-pcs.com/printable/details.html

[12] http://www.life-enthusiast.com/megahydrate-and-your-health-a-336.html

[13] http://www.ncbi.nlm.nih.gov/pubmed/23930027

[14] http://soushrutam.com/010203.pdf

[15] https://deltaaware.files.wordpress.com/2014/04/slid e11.png